THE EXPERT WITNES

The Expert Witness in Court

A Practical Guide

Catherine Bond
Mark Solon
Penny Harper

Shaw & Sons

Published by
Shaw & Sons Limited
Shaway House
21 Bourne Park
Bourne Road
Crayford
Kent DA1 4BZ

© Shaw & Sons Limited 1997

Published November 1997

ISBN 0 7219 1440 3

A CIP catalogue record for this book is available from
the British Library

Printed in Great Britain by
Biddles Limited, Guildford

CONTENTS

The Authors

All three are solicitors and trainers of expert witnesses. Catherine Bond has worked with Withers and Wilde Sapte in the City and Crowell & Moring in the United States. Penny Harper has worked with Kingsley Napley in London and is a senior lecturer with the College of Law. Mark Solon has worked with Clyde & Co in the City and had his own practice, Young & Solon for 10 years in London. He is also qualified in the United States.

Bond Solon Training

Bond Solon Training has developed a programme of courses specifically designed to develop the essential skills required for the second role as an expert witness. We take for granted the first role. Expert witnesses who participate in this programme will become as professional in their role as expert witnesses as in their role as professionals in their chosen field.

The courses are very intensive with small numbers of delegates. They are short to avoid taking time from other activities. They are an excellent investment for all experts, from those of many years' standing, to those who have just taken their first case. We have trained over 7,000 experts in the skills needed to produce first-class written and oral evidence.

Enquiries to 0171-925 0330.

Access to Justice – the Lord Woolf Enquiry

Lord Woolf, the Master of the Rolls, was assigned to report to the Lord Chancellor on the civil justice system in England and Wales. He delivered his final report in July 1996. There is some uncertainty at present as to the extent to which his recommendations will be implemented by the Labour government but we have made reference to the recommendations where appropriate. The reader will need to keep track of the progress of their implementation.

There is a summary of the recommendations and the text relating to experts in Appendix 3.

Chapter 1

EXPERT EVIDENCE IN CONTEXT

SUMMARY

- The English legal system •
- Who is who in the legal system •

The criminal courts

- Court structure •
- The personnel •
- The parties •
- The burden of proof •
- How criminal cases start •
- Evidence in criminal trials •
- Witnesses in criminal trials •
- The role of the expert in a criminal trial •
- Procedure of a criminal trial •

The civil courts

- Court structure •
- The personnel •
- The parties •
- The burden of proof •
- How civil cases start and proceed •
- Evidence in civil trials •
- Witnesses in civil trials •
- The role of experts and expert reports •

The English Legal System

There are two types of cases within the English legal system. These are **Criminal Cases**, where the state takes action against an individual to determine if that individual is guilty or not guilty of a crime, and **Civil Cases** which involve one individual taking action against another, usually to get money. There are accordingly different courts and procedures depending on whether a case is a criminal case or a civil case.

A broad overview of the court system is set out below. In addition, there are also numerous tribunals such as Industrial Tribunals, Immigration Tribunals and so on.

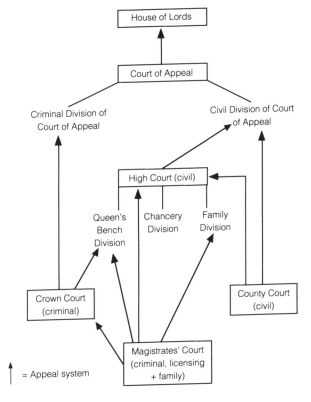

THE ADVERSARIAL SYSTEM

In both civil and criminal cases in the United Kingdom, there is an adversarial system.

Two parties come before the court; their version of events is in dispute. They are usually represented by lawyers who argue or advocate their case. The court must find out what happened, taking into account evidence of facts and evidence of opinion. Facts are what someone saw, heard or did. Opinion evidence is given by expert witnesses. The opinion expressed is an independent view of the facts which the expert gives to help the lawyers and the court to understand what the case is about. Experts' qualifications and experience enable them to form such an opinion. For example, a surveyor might say that cracks in a wall did not arise as a result of subsidence.

Each party, usually represented by its lawyers, is entitled to call its own evidence. Each party also has the opportunity to cross-examine, by means of critical questions, the evidence of its opponent's witnesses. The court will also look at other evidence such as documentary evidence or real evidence, for example the knife used to commit a killing.

The adversarial system represents a fight between the two parties. The lawyers represent their clients and they fight to win. Each side may have its own expert witnesses and sometimes a court expert is appointed, as recommended by the Woolf Report (see Appendix 3, page 143).

It is important for experts to be independent. They should not succumb to the wishes of the lawyers who are paid to win the cases. The role of experts is that of independent educators; they are there to assist the court to reach a fair decision.

THE LEGAL PROFESSION – WHO'S WHO?

Solicitors

Solicitors form partnerships or work as sole traders to provide legal services, from offices. They are available to give advice directly to members of the public. The professional body for solicitors is The Law Society.

Solicitors are responsible for the whole case management, for example advising the client, arranging meetings with barristers, preparing documents for court and negotiating settlement of the case. Thus the day to day running of the case is done by solicitors. It is the solicitors who instruct experts and an expert witness should work with the solicitors to educate them in the area of the expert's specialisation.

Solicitors have rights of audience in the Magistrates' Court, the County Court and sometimes in the Crown Court and High Court.

Barrister/Counsel

Barristers work on an individual self-employed basis. Members of the public cannot go directly to barristers for advice. Barristers are instructed by solicitors and sometimes other professions to give advice on points of law and procedures and to represent members of the public in court. The solicitors send barristers documents which summarise what it is that the solicitor wants the barrister to do; these documents are called briefs. Barristers have rights of audience, meaning they can represent a client, in all the courts. They wear wigs and gowns in court. They share offices called "chambers" with other barristers.

"Conference with counsel" is a meeting in which barristers give advice. Solicitors and their clients and experts attend such conferences. Experts can use these meetings to help barristers to understand the issues and see the strengths and weaknesses highlighted by the expert opinion.

Q.C.s/Silks/Leading Counsel

A Q.C. is a senior barrister with usually at least 20 years' experience or "call" as a barrister. Junior Counsel is a barrister of any number of years' experience, who has not become a Q.C. In many cases it will only be necessary to have one barrister, a Junior Counsel.

Training of Solicitors and Barristers

Both solicitors and barristers study law degrees or do a non-law degree followed by an intensive year of legal studies for the Common Professional Exam (CPE). After this they make a personal choice as to whether they want to be solicitors or barristers. Those who want to become solicitors take a further one year's study with exams, called the Legal Practice Course (LPC); they must then do two years in a solicitors firm in a training contract before they qualify as solicitors. Those who want to become barristers do one year's study on a Bar Vocational Course with exams. When they have passed these exams, they can then call themselves barristers. However, to practise as a self-employed barrister they must undertake one year's pupillage, where they learn from a senior barrister.

Legal Executives

Legal executives are employed in solicitors firms to do some of the more routine work. They often do not have degrees. They may start work with a law firm after leaving school and learn on the job. They also take some exams in law with the Institute of Legal Executives (ILEX).

The Crown Prosecution Service (CPS)

This is staffed by lawyers who are paid by the state to prosecute criminal cases. In Magistrates' Courts lawyers working for the CPS usually represent the prosecution. However, they do not yet have the right to appear in the Crown Court. This means that, in the Crown Court, the prosecution will always be represented by a barrister instructed by the CPS.

Judges

There are many different sorts of judges. They are independent and listen to both parties in any dispute before making a decision to resolve the dispute. Judges are employed by the State.

The Criminal Courts

The vast majority of criminal cases are brought against a defendant by the State, although occasionally there are private prosecutions. The Crown Prosecution Service (CPS) is usually responsible for the prosecution of the defendant.

COURT STRUCTURE

Magistrates' Court

All criminal cases have initial proceedings in the Magistrates' Court and over 90% are completed there. The magistrates will decide whether a defendant is to be held in custody to await trial – the court hearing – at which it will be decided if the defendant is guilty or not guilty, or whether the defendant will be granted bail and released on the condition that they return to court on a particular date. They also decide if a defendant is entitled to legal aid. Finally they may have to decide whether the defendant's trial will take place in the Magistrates' Court or in the Crown Court (see flow diagram on page 14).

Criminal trials that take place in the Magistrates' Court are called **summary trials**. Summary trials are used to try the less serious crimes, for example minor road traffic offences such as speeding, driving without a licence or careless driving; cases of shoplifting, theft of small amounts, minor offences against the person or against property are also commonly dealt with by summary trial. 95% of criminal trials are summary trials.

A summary trial will be heard by the magistrates who will decide if the defendant is guilty or not guilty. A psychologist may be involved in giving opinion on whether a defendant is fit to give evidence at trial. The magistrates will also pass sentence but, in some cases, they can send the defendant to Crown Court for sentencing if they consider their own powers of sentencing are inadequate and a higher penalty is required. They will often adjourn to get pre-sentence reports by the Probation Service before passing sentence. An expert, for example a psychiatrist, may be involved in helping to prepare a pre-sentence report. This report is used to help decide which sentence is most suitable.

Who Sits (Makes the Decision)

There will usually be three lay magistrates on the "bench". These will be three non-lawyers who have volunteered to sit as Justices of the Peace. They will be assisted in matters of law and practice by a legally qualified Magistrate's Clerk. Sometimes, instead of three lay magistrates there will be one stipendiary magistrate sitting alone. The stipendiary magistrate will be a qualified barrister or solicitor with at least seven years' experience.

Correct Form of Address

Magistrates should be addressed as "Sir" or "Madam".

The Crown Court

The Crown Court tries the more serious crimes. Trial in the Crown Court is known as trial on **indictment**. The indictment sets out the charges against the defendant. The sorts of case that will be heard in the Crown Court are murder, rape, fraud, drug offences, robbery, burglary, serious offences against persons and property, dangerous driving.

The Crown Court also hears appeals from the Magistrates' Court and cases in which the magistrates have committed the defendant for sentence.

Who Sits

Crown Court trials are jury trials, presided over by a judge who may be a High Court judge, a circuit judge or a recorder. The judge directs the jury on the law and on the weight to be attached to the evidence of each witness. The jury decides whether the defendant is guilty or not guilty. If the defendant is convicted, the judge passes sentence, usually after an adjournment for pre-sentence reports.

Correct Form of Address

This depends on the status of the judge. Ask the usher or the lawyers. All judges sitting in the Crown Court (circuit judges, recorders and assistant recorders) are addressed as "Your Honour" except High Court (or red) judges and any judge sitting at the Old Bailey in London or in the Court of the Recorder of Liverpool or Manchester. These judges are all addressed as "Your Lordship/ Ladyship" or "My Lord/Lady". A High Court judge is often referred to as a "red judge" because their formal court attire is coloured red (and black). On the court list, a High Court judge's surname is always followed by the abbreviation "J.", as opposed to the abbreviation "H.H.J." used for circuit judges.

The High Court

Appeals from the Magistrates' Court or the Crown Court may sometimes be heard in the Queen's Bench Division of the High Court.

Who Sits

One High Court judge and one Lord Justice of Appeal.

Correct Form of Address

"Your Lordship/Ladyship" or "My Lord/Lady".

The Court of Appeal

The Criminal Division hears appeals from the Crown Court on points of law and also appeals against sentence by the prosecution or the defence.

Who Sits

Usually three, but sometimes two, judges. At least one of these judges must be a Lord Justice of Appeal. The other judges may be either two further Lords Justices of Appeal, two High Court judges or one High Court judge and one circuit judge. The Lord Chief Justice is a Lord Justice of Appeal. He is also the head of the Criminal Division of the Supreme Court and is the most senior criminal judge in England and Wales.

Correct Form of Address

"Your Lordship/Ladyship" or "My Lord/Lady".

The House of Lords

Like the Court of Appeal, the House of Lords is exclusively appellate. It hears appeals from the Court of Appeal (Criminal Division) and also (exceptionally) from the Queen's Bench Division of the High Court.

Who Sits

From three to seven, but usually five, Lords of Appeal.

Correct Form of Address

"Your Lordship/Ladyship" or "My Lord/Lady".

PARTIES TO PROCEEDINGS IN THE CRIMINAL COURTS

The Prosecution

The State/Crown, through the Crown Prosecution Service, prosecute people for allegedly committing crimes. Examples of such crimes are fraud, theft, burglary, robbery, rape, assaults against the person, murder, manslaughter, dangerous diving, drug smuggling, etc. Exceptionally, an individual victim may bring a private prosecution.

At the trial, the prosecution's case against the defendant is heard first.

The Defence

The defendant in a criminal trial is the person whom the prosecution alleges has committed a criminal offence. Criminal offences are set out in statutes, i.e. Acts of Parliament, or exist as common law offences, that is they are offences that have been created by judges in decided cases. The defendant may be found "guilty" or "not guilty". This is a decision made by the jury in the Crown Court and by the magistrates in the Magistrates' Court. Sentences may be custodial or non-custodial, i.e. the defendant can be imprisoned or given a sentence falling short of imprisonment such as a fine or a community sentence.

THE BURDEN AND STANDARD OF PROOF

Generally the burden or onus of proof rests on the prosecution. They have to show that there is sufficient evidence to convict the defendant. The prosecution is required to prove every fact in issue to a high standard, that is beyond reasonable doubt, in order to secure a conviction.

This burden extends not only to proving every element of the offence but also to disproving the defendant's defence. The aim is to get to the truth of what happened. This means that, in situations where the defendant wishes to rely on a defence such as self-defence, provocation or duress, it is for the prosecution to disprove these defences beyond reasonable doubt.

There are a few occasions where the burden of proof falls on the defence. For example, where the defendant wishes to plead insanity or diminished responsibility, the defence must prove it. However, the defence is only required to prove such a defence on the balance of probability (rather than beyond reasonable doubt).

When the prosecution must prove their case beyond reasonable doubt, the jury or magistrates should convict only if they are sure that the defendant is guilty. By contrast, where the defence is required to prove its defence on the balance of probability, the jury or magistrates should accept this defence only if they are satisfied that the defence is more likely to be true than not.

HOW CRIMINAL CASES START

Investigation and prosecution of criminal cases is funded by the State. Criminal cases start with an investigation by the police, Customs and Excise, the Serious Fraud Office (S.F.O.) or the Department of Trade and Industry (D.T.I.). If, after investigation, it is believed that an individual has committed an offence, then one of two courses will be followed.

In cases where it is not deemed necessary to arrest the offender, a summons is served advising them that it is believed that they have committed a criminal offence. Alternatively, the individual will be arrested and then, usually after a police interview, will be formally charged. In each case they will then be committed to court to be tried.

Offences are classified into three types in criminal proceedings: summary, "either way" and indictable. Trials of summary only offences, that is less serious offences, always take place in the Magistrates' Court. Trials of indictable only offences, the most serious offences such as murder, take place in the Crown Court.

Trials of "either way" offences such as theft may, however, take place in either the Crown Court or the Magistrates' Court. The magistrates decide at a Mode of Trial hearing whether the case is suitable to be tried in the Magistrates' Court or in the Crown Court. If the former, the magistrates will continue with the hearing to try the offence.

When the Magistrates' Court decides that an "either way" offence is to be tried at the Crown Court, and in the case of all indictable only offences, there will be a **committal** hearing in the Magistrates' Court. This is a hearing to send the defendant to the Crown Court for trial, if the prosecution have sufficient evidence for there to be a "case to answer", that is that there is sufficient prosecution evidence to warrant the case being listed for trial in the Crown Court.

Thus the initial proceedings for all cases take place in the Magistrates' Court.

A full trial of indictable only offences and "either way" offences committed to the Crown Court will take place at Crown Court unless the defendant pleads guilty. If the defendant pleads guilty, the Crown Court will move on to consider sentencing. If the defendant pleads not guilty but is found guilty, sentencing will usually take place on a different day.

The magistrates decide if a defendant is entitled to be released on bail pending trial, or whether the defendant will be held in custody to await trial. They also decide if the defendant is entitled to have legal aid to defend the case. This decision will be based partly on the means of the defendant and partly on whether it is in the "interests of justice" that the defendant should receive legal aid.

Appeals may be made to the higher courts from the Magistrates' Court or the Crown Court. The following diagram shows the full procedure in criminal cases, including the appeals structure.

Criminal Litigation: An Overview of the Procedure and Appeal System

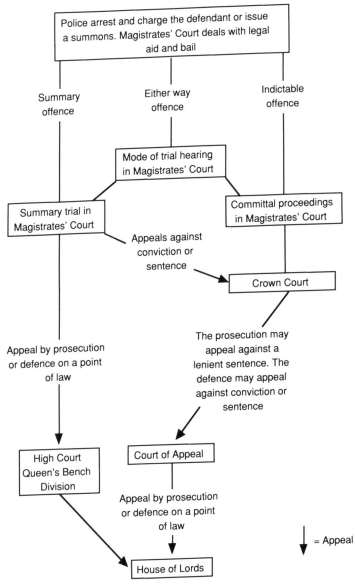

Police arrest and charge the defendant or issue a summons. Magistrates' Court deals with legal aid and bail

Summary offence

Either way offence

Indictable offence

Mode of trial hearing in Magistrates' Court

Summary trial in Magistrates' Court

Committal proceedings in Magistrates' Court

Appeals against conviction or sentence

Crown Court

Appeal by prosecution or defence on a point of law

The prosecution may appeal against a lenient sentence. The defence may appeal against conviction or sentence

High Court Queen's Bench Division

Court of Appeal

Appeal by prosecution or defence on a point of law

House of Lords

= Appeal

EVIDENCE IN CRIMINAL TRIALS

The key to the adversarial system is the testing of evidence. This allows the court to decide how much weight or credit to attach to each piece of evidence.

There are many detailed rules of evidence. An expert does not need to know all these and should feel free to ask the lawyers which rules are relevant. There are, however, some rules which it is useful to understand.

Evidence can be divided into three categories: documentary evidence, real evidence and witness evidence.

Documentary evidence includes such things as photographs, photofits, and video and tape recordings. Documents have to be proved to be authentic which means that a witness may have to be called to give oral evidence to explain how a document came into existence.

Examples of real evidence are a knife, a gun and a piece of paper with the defendant's signature on.

Discovery/Disclosure of Evidence

Disclosure of evidence means letting the other party know what evidence you have.

A party to criminal proceedings in the Crown Court who is going to call expert evidence at trial is required to give advance disclosure of the content of this evidence to all other parties. This disclosure must be given after committal to the Crown Court for trial. If such advance disclosure is not given, then the oral or written evidence of the expert cannot be given at Crown Court without the leave (permission) of the judge. A judge will only grant leave if he or she thinks it is fair to do so.

If the trial is in the Magistrates' Court, there is not a formal obligation to give advance disclosure of expert evidence to any other party. However, it will often be disclosed to avoid an opponent having to ask for an adjournment during the trial to get their own expert opinion.

Witness Summons/Subpoena

A witness summons is a written order from the court demanding the attendance of a witness.

Witnesses will be asked to confirm in writing that they will attend court to give oral evidence at a trial. If no reply is received or if the witness refuses to attend, then the solicitor will write to the court explaining that they have not been able to secure voluntary attendance of a witness. To make sure the witness comes to court, the court will order them to by issuing a witness summons.

The solicitor for either party to a case can apply to the court for a witness summons to be issued to each witness, whether an expert witness or a witness as to fact, who is required to give oral evidence at court and will not otherwise attend. A witness summons will be served personally on the witness. It will tell the witness where and when they must go. If a witness fails to attend after receiving a witness summons they may be arrested, brought to court and fined and/or imprisoned as a punishment for their failure to comply with the summons.

As far as witness evidence is concerned, there are three types of witnesses: witnesses of fact, professional witnesses and expert witnesses.

WITNESSES OF FACT

A witness of fact is someone who is called to give evidence about what happened in a case. They are there to recall what they saw or heard during an incident but not to give opinions. They are required to discuss the facts they remember or recorded in notes. Examples of such witnesses are a witness to a fight; a nurse in a hospital who saw a patient in casualty and recorded details of their injuries; a police officer who made notes in his/her notebook; a witness who gives identification evidence.

A witness as to fact *must* give oral evidence at the trial unless the opposing party agrees that the witness's statement may be read instead. They may only testify to those things that they heard or saw themselves and not to anything that they were told happened by a third party. Such "second hand" evidence is classified as hearsay and is not admissible.

While in the witness box, a witness may refresh their memory from any contemporaneous records they have kept. Contemporaneous records are records completed while the facts were still fresh in the witness's mind. Such a contemporaneous note may be read out by the witness as part of the oral evidence. The note may be questioned and inspected by the "opposing" party to the trial.

Examples of such notes are a police officer's notebook, a scientist's record of experiments into drugs, chemicals or handwriting, and medical records. It is important to keep accurate full notes containing the following type of information:

— Dates, start and finish time, location.

— Who was present, e.g. researcher, patient, client.

— Examination/experiment and finding.

— Details of facts observed and opinions (the latter if you will be an expert witness as well as a witness as to fact).

— Details of advice given/conversations.

A witness as to fact is not entitled to sit in court and listen to other witnesses' evidence before they give their evidence.

Witness of Fact Statement in Criminal Trials

Witnesses of fact do not write reports but make statements.

A statement will usually be written some time after the event to which it refers and usually at the prompting of a police officer or a solicitor. Its purpose is to set out in writing the witness's recollection of the events in question in as much detail as possible using the witness's memory and/or notes taken at the time. The statement itself is *not* the witness's evidence. This evidence is given orally from the witness box. Generally the witness is *not* allowed to take a witness statement into the witness box but, as seen above, they can take contemporaneous notes. Sometimes the witness statement is comprised entirely of contemporaneous notes and the witness may therefore be allowed to take it into the witness box.

A witness statement which is not contemporaneous is used both to refresh the witness's memory outside the witness box and to allow both parties to see what the witness's evidence is prior to trial. There must be no ambush evidence.

In the following situations, the witness statement can be used as evidence *without* the need to call the witness to give oral evidence.

1. As a section 9 statement under the Criminal Justice Act 1967. This is where a signed witness statement, which has been served on the other party in advance of the trial, can be admitted as evidence because the other party has read it and has

decided they do not wish to cross-examine the witness and they do not object to the witness statement being read in court. In this case there is no need for the witness to give oral evidence in the witness box. This procedure is commonly used where the witness merely gives formal evidence, for example a relative of the deceased identifying the body in a murder case. But if the other party does object to the section 9 statement being read out, the witness must give oral evidence. The purpose of a section 9 statement is to avoid the time and expense of a witness going to court when this is unnecessary.

The declaration at the top of a section 9 statement reads "This statement, consisting of x pages, is true to the best of my knowledge and belief and I make it knowing that, if it is tendered in evidence, I shall be liable to prosecution if I have wilfully stated in it anything which I know to be false or do not believe to be true."

2. The statement was made by someone who is now dead, or unfit to attend as a witness, or is outside the United Kingdom and it is not reasonably practicable to secure their attendance, or the statement was made to the police and the person refuses to give evidence through fear.

3. The witness has recorded observations in a business document or record of accounts or they are stored in a computer.

Do Witnesses of Fact Get Paid?

Witnesses of fact do not get paid for giving evidence but they may claim their travelling expenses. A number of people give factual evidence as part of their job, for example police officers and traffic wardens.

EXPERT WITNESSES

An expert witness will give evidence of both **facts** and **opinion**.

Evidence of Facts

Facts fall into two different categories.

1. There are those facts which the expert has observed himself, such as handwriting, a concrete base, a broken leg, skid marks on a road.

2. There are those facts that an expert has been told, such as the level of pain, mental injury caused, the distance from which a rifle was fired, or facts observed from documents or real evidence. Included in this category of facts are facts that have been reported to the expert by a member of his/her research team.

The facts which will be given most weight by the court will be those observed by experts themselves. However, the court is allowed to take into account other facts which experts have relied on to come to their expert opinion. Of course most of the facts relied on will have to be tested by the oral cross-examination of witnesses as to fact. The expert should clearly identify the source of the facts, e.g. "I have been told by Mr. X that ..." or "At about 11.00 a.m. on 10th July 1997 at Greenway Police Station I examined the accused and I saw that he had bruising around the left eye."

Evidence of Opinion

Expert opinion evidence is admissible on matters not within the common knowledge of the court. The reason for an expert witness being asked to give evidence is because the court does not know or understand matters within certain fields. They need the help of an expert to understand the case. Experts are entitled to give opinion evidence because of their qualifications and experience in their particular field of expertise. For example, a scientist who examines a suspicious substance may say that in his expert opinion it has all the characteristics of cannabis. Expertise may exist in a wide range of fields including medicine, science, technology, environmental issues, pension funds, loss of earnings, etc.

The Role of the Expert Witness

In criminal trials expert witnesses will often be giving their opinion on whether or not the defendant was involved in the offence or any element of it. It is essential for the expert witness to know what offence the defendant is charged with and what the likely defence is.

For example, in a robbery, where the defendant is putting forward a defence that he or she was not at the scene of the crime, a forensic scientist may be giving evidence of their own analysis of the D.N.A. found in hairs collected at the scene of the crime, and may say that, in their opinion, this analysis shows that it is statistically probable that the defendant was at the scene of the crime.

A psychiatrist or a psychologist may give evidence as to what type of sentence is most appropriate for the defendant following the defendant's conviction.

In a murder case, a doctor may give medical evidence on whether or not the defendant had a state of mind which a jury could find amounted to a defence of diminished responsibility or insanity.

Remember, an expert witness gives evidence of both fact and opinion. For instance, in the D.N.A example above, the evidence about the carrying out of the D.N.A. analysis and its results is evidence of *fact*, whereas the evidence about the statistical probability of the defendant being present at the scene is *opinion* evidence. Opinion evidence must be based on a foundation of factual evidence.

Expert Reports

Experts will generally write a report, unlike witnesses as to fact and professional witnesses who make statements. A report is a written document which sets out what the facts are and what the expert's opinion is. Chapter 3 deals with the writing of experts' reports and there is an example of an expert's report in the appendices.

It is possible for the court to read an expert's written report even though the expert does not attend the trial, if the other party agrees it is not necessary for the expert to give oral evidence or the court gives leave for the report to be admissible without the expert's attendance. However, a court usually gives more weight to the expert's evidence when the expert attends the trial and gives evidence orally and that evidence is subjected to rigorous testing under cross-examination.

An expert is entitled to take their report into the witness box and refer to it while giving evidence. They should have a clean copy of the report and should not take in an annotated copy.

Privilege for Expert's Report Prepared for the Defendant

Privilege means that a report is protected from public general knowledge. The existence and content of the report can only be known to the expert, the instructing solicitor and the solicitor's client.

Communications between a defendant or their solicitor and an expert are privileged, so long as they were made in contemplation of pending litigation. If a document (for example a letter, a record of a telephone call, or a draft or final version of an expert's report) is privileged, then the defence cannot be compelled to reveal it to the prosecution. An expert's report that is unfavourable to the accused and is not going to be used at trial need never be disclosed, that is revealed, to the other party(ies).

Discovery/Disclosure of Expert's Report Prepared for the Defendant

There is a general rule that trials cannot be conducted by ambush, so once a party decides it is going to rely on a piece of evidence at trial, it must be revealed to the other side. At this stage, known as disclosure, the privilege over the report is lost. The report is disclosed or revealed to the other side.

If an expert report is going to be relied on by the defence at the Crown Court, it must be disclosed to the prosecution. Once the defence has disclosed an expert's report to the prosecution (whether the case is to be heard in the Crown Court or in the Magistrates' Court), the defence is deemed to have waived the privilege in the report. In the Magistrates' Court it is usual for the defence to disclose all the experts' reports on which they propose to rely well in advance of the trial. This avoids the trial court having to grant the prosecution an adjournment during the trial in order to give the prosecution the opportunity to deal with this expert evidence (by instructing and calling an expert of its own).

Under the Crown Court (Advance Notice of Expert Evidence) Rules 1987, both prosecution and defence must provide each other with expert evidence to be relied on at trial and, on request, provide supporting evidence. There should be no surprise evidence.

- Note that any records or accounts that were prepared for reasons other than litigation do not enjoy privilege and are liable to be disclosed to the other side.

- The duty on the prosecution to disclose unused/unfavourable evidence is more onerous than on the defence.

PROFESSIONAL WITNESSES

Most professional witnesses give evidence as a result of seeing something happen in the course of their everyday job. Giving evidence about it is also part of their job. The best examples are police officers and police surgeons.

Professional witnesses can give some opinion evidence. However, they often give a lot of factual evidence. Their evidence is in the form of a statement, not a report. If the evidence they give is not disputed by the other party, it may be given as a section 9 statement. This means the evidence will be read in court without the need for them to give oral evidence.

Professional witnesses are classified separately for purposes of payment of fees only.

PROCEDURE OF A CRIMINAL TRIAL

1. Prosecution opening speech.

2. Prosecution call their evidence first.

   For each witness: Examination in chief (by prosecution)

   Cross-examination (by defence)

   Re-examination (by prosecution).

3. At the end of the prosecution case, the defence may make a submission of "no case to answer" if the prosecution evidence cannot be relied on and they cannot prove key elements of the offence charged. If the court agrees there is no case to answer, the defendant will be set free. If there is a case to answer then:

4. Defence opening speech.

5. Defence call their evidence.

For each witness: Examination in chief (by defence)

Cross-examination (by prosecution)

Re-examination (by defence).

6. Defence closing speech.

Prosecution may have a closing speech (in Crown Court but rarely in Magistrates Court).

In a criminal trial, the witnesses of fact may not sit in court and listen to other witnesses' evidence before they give their own evidence. However, expert witnesses may sit in court and listen to all the evidence.

The Civil Courts

COURT STRUCTURE

There are two civil courts in which cases are commenced and trials are held, the County Court and the High Court. However, it should be noted that the vast majority of civil litigation cases (96%) are settled before they come to trial.

Proceedings in respect of personal injury litigation must be commenced in the County Court, unless the value of the action is £50,000 or more in which case proceedings may be started in the High Court. However, there is no limit to the damages that can be awarded in the County Court. In practice, therefore, most personal injury actions are started in the County Court even if they are worth more than £50,000.

In relation to other types of action, there is a choice as to whether the action is started in the County Court or the High Court.

As far as the venue for *trial* is concerned, the presumption is that where the value of the action exceeds £50,000 it will be heard in the High Court. Where the value of the action is less than £25,000, the presumption is that the action will be tried in the County Court. There is no such presumption for actions with a value of between £25,000 and £50,000. These are only presumptions; the actual venue for trial depends on a number of other factors such as the factual and legal complexity of the action and its importance to the public at large.

The County Court

The sort of cases held in the County Court are building disputes, claims for faulty goods, personal injury litigation, landlord and tenant litigation, and professional negligence.

Who Sits

Trials in which the sum in issue is less than £5,000 are heard by a district judge. Actions where the sum in issue is more than £5,000 are heard by a circuit judge, recorder or assistant recorder.

Correct Form of Address

A district judge, recorder and assistant recorder are addressed as "Sir" or "Madam". A circuit judge is addressed as "Your Honour".

The Small Claims Court

The Small Claims Court is part of the County Court which deals with claims not exceeding £3,000 (or £1,000 if personal injury). Cases are heard at an informal hearing before a district judge. Legal aid is not available and the "loser" of the litigation is not liable for paying the "winner's" costs.

Arbitration

Arbitration is an adjudication process operating outside the court process in which a third party will reach a decision which is binding on the parties. Arbitration is automatically imposed in civil proceedings started in the County Court where the amount of the claim does not exceed £1,000 and a defence to the claim is filed. Procedure at arbitration hearings is less formal and the arbitration can avoid long delays before reaching a solution. Expert witnesses and other witnesses will give evidence. The disadvantage of arbitration is that legal aid is not available for the hearing itself. The successful party can only recover the costs of taking out the summons and the cost of entering the award of damages; the costs of instructing a solicitor are not recoverable. Parties in disputes of a value higher than £1,000 may agree to arbitration and chose their own arbitrator. The arbitrator chosen may in fact be an expert in a particular field, who will understand the issues at stake. For example, a construction engineer may be the arbitrator in a building dispute. The decision of the arbitrator is binding on the parties.

Alternative Dispute Resolution (ADR)

This is an alternative to litigation through the civil court system. The purpose of ADR is to enable parties to settle their disputes outside the courtroom by using a third party to act as a mediator. This mediator does not give a binding judgment; it is up to the parties to negotiate a settlement. If they are unable to negotiate an agreement, the parties can proceed to arbitration.

The advantage of ADR is that it is quicker, cheaper and less formal than court proceedings. It is suitable for parties who wish to retain a working relationship after the dispute is over.

Sometimes a contract between two parties will provide for ADR in the event of a contractual dispute. Alternatively, the parties can simply agree to use ADR instead of litigation through the court system.

The High Court

The High Court has three divisions:

(i) Queen's Bench Division (includes the Commercial Court and the Admiralty Court) – breach of contract, negligence and judicial review are the main claims.

(ii) Chancery Division (includes the Companies Court and the Patents Court) – trusts, probate, land disputes, partnership action.

(iii) Family Division – wardship, adoption, guardianship.

Who Sits

Usually one High Court judge, but it can be a circuit judge or senior Q.C.

In cases of libel, slander, malicious prosecution and unlawful imprisonment, a *jury* will usually sit with the judge. The jury will make the decisions of fact; the judge will direct the proceedings.

Correct Form of Address

"Your Lordship/Ladyship" or "My Lord/Lady".

The Court of Appeal (Civil Division)

Few civil cases go to the Court of Appeal. Appeals are heard from the High Court, the County Court and certain tribunals. The jurisdiction is entirely appellate. Documents will be read and legal argument presented. The decision may be by a majority.

Who Sits

Three Lords Justice of Appeal. These may include the Lord Chief Justice, the Master of the Rolls or the Vice Chancellor.

Correct Form of Address

"Your Lordship/Ladyship" or "My Lord/Lady".

The House of Lords

Sits in the committee rooms in the Houses of Parliament at Westminster.

The House of Lords only hears cases where there is a principle of law that is of great public importance. The House of Lords listens to legal argument.

Who Sits

Between three and seven, but usually five, Lords of Appeal will sit. Sometimes the Lord Chancellor will preside.

Correct Form of Address

"Your Lordship/Ladyship" or "My Lord/Lady".

Magistrates' Court

Generally, Magistrates' Courts deal with criminal cases but they also deal with family matters and licensing.

Correct Form of Address

"Sir/Madam".

Tribunals

There are many separate tribunals which hear specialist cases within the civil justice system. For example, there are industrial tribunals which hear disputes about employment law rights and issues, social security tribunals and immigration tribunals. Proceedings in tribunals are less formal than in court. There is usually a panel of three people (one of whom is usually a lawyer) who decide the cases. Witnesses usually sit down to give their evidence.

PARTIES TO THE PROCEEDINGS IN THE CIVIL COURTS

Litigation is between the plaintiff and the defendant. Each party sets out their case in writing ("pleadings"). These pleadings set out the details of what happened, what evidence the party has and what the party wants.

The Plaintiff

A plaintiff is someone who starts a court action. Usually, they believe that they have suffered a wrongful loss. For example, they believe that the other party to a contract has broken it, or they have been physically injured in a road traffic accident or have been given poor professional advice. The plaintiff wants to claim money from the person or organisation who caused the loss and brings a court action (sues) to obtain financial compensation in the form of *damages* from a defendant.

Most plaintiffs instruct lawyers to help them bring their case. There are two things that the plaintiff has to show to the court:

1. That the defendant, the person being sued, is responsible for the plaintiff's loss or damage. This is known as liability.

2. If liability can be established, the *amount* of money that is due (this is called *quantum*, a Latin word meaning amount). The amount of money awarded is to compensate the plaintiff (as far as money can) for their loss.

Expert witnesses may be asked to give their opinion on either liability or quantum or both.

For example, a surveyor may be asked to give an opinion as to the cause of a roof collapsing; whether it was due to adverse weather conditions or inadequate support beams in the roof (liability). He or she may also be asked to give his/her opinion on the amount of damages (quantum) the plaintiff should recover to compensate the plaintiff for the collapsed roof. The surveyor may be asked to estimate how much it will cost the plaintiff to rebuild the roof.

At the trial, the plaintiff's case will be heard first.

The Defendant

The defendant is a person or organisation from whom money is claimed, for example a motorist who has run over a pedestrian and injured him. The compensation is called damages. If the plaintiff wins the case, then an order to pay damages will be made. The losing defendant is not "guilty", but merely said to be liable to the plaintiff and judgment is entered against them. When the defendant is insured, the defence will usually be run by the insurance company.

THE BURDEN AND STANDARD OF PROOF

The burden of proving a fact lies with the party bringing the action, the plaintiff. So, if a plaintiff is alleging professional negligence, then the plaintiff must prove all the elements of the tort of negligence. The issues that arise are:

(i) That duty of care existed between the plaintiff and the defendant.

(ii) That the defendant breached this duty of care.

(iii) That the breach *caused* the plaintiff loss/damage.

(iv) The amount of this loss/damage.

In civil cases, the plaintiff is required to prove a fact on the balance of probabilities. This is an easier burden than the "beyond reasonable doubt" required in criminal cases. It means that the judge must be persuaded that the plaintiff's version of events is more likely to be true than the defendant's.

Civil Litigation: Overview of the Procedure

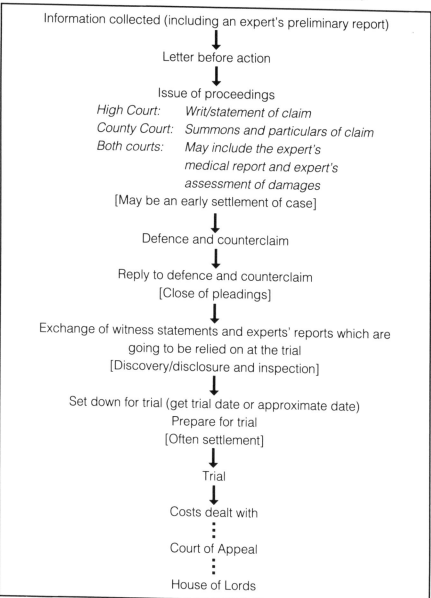

Information collected (including an expert's preliminary report)

↓

Letter before action

↓

Issue of proceedings

High Court: *Writ/statement of claim*
County Court: *Summons and particulars of claim*
Both courts: *May include the expert's*
medical report and expert's
assessment of damages

[May be an early settlement of case]

↓

Defence and counterclaim

↓

Reply to defence and counterclaim
[Close of pleadings]

↓

Exchange of witness statements and experts' reports which are
going to be relied on at the trial
[Discovery/disclosure and inspection]

↓

Set down for trial (get trial date or approximate date)
Prepare for trial
[Often settlement]

↓

Trial

↓

Costs dealt with

⋮

Court of Appeal

⋮

House of Lords

HOW CIVIL CASES START

The Expert's Role

Before starting a civil case, the solicitors instructed by the plaintiff will have to establish that it is worthwhile to bring the case. The plaintiff's solicitors will collect as much information as they can about what happened.

An expert witness has an important role to play at this stage. Expert witnesses will often be asked to provide a **"preliminary report"** by the solicitors. This is to help the solicitors to decide if the plaintiff has a case worth bringing against the defendant. The solicitors will also have obtained statements from witnesses as to fact who saw and heard the incident in question.

It is important that the expert witness exercises clear, independent judgement when writing a preliminary report. The solicitor needs to know all the weaknesses of the case as well as the strengths. If the expert writes an unfavourable report, then the solicitor may advise the client not to start litigation.

If the client still wishes to go ahead with litigation, there will be no need for the expert's unfavourable report to be revealed to the other side. This is because only an expert's report that the party is going to rely on at trial will have to be disclosed to the other side. Unfavourable reports which are not used remain privileged, that is they remain confidential to the client, the expert and the client's solicitor.

Many different types of experts may be used in civil litigation, e.g. engineers, psychologists, psychiatrists, doctors, scientists, accountants, surveyors, etc.

PRE-ACTION DISCOVERY AND INSPECTION

Before the case is formally started in court, each side may need to know what documents, notes, photographs, etc. the other side has. They may need pre-action discovery, that is to know of the existence of documents which the other party has in their custody, possession or control. A list of any such evidence is made available by both sides. An expert may need to see these documents. A party may also need pre-action inspection (the right to see) of the property of the other party or a third party. Again, the expert may need to see this and to take photographs, etc. Court orders are needed for pre-action discovery or inspection if this is not given voluntarily.

An expert will often have to make arrangements to see a patient, or visit the scene of an accident to do sketches and take photographs.

ISSUE OF PROCEEDINGS

The issue of proceedings is the formal process by which litigation is started in the court system. Before issuing proceedings, the plaintiff's solicitor will send a "letter before action". This will threaten to start litigation unless a settlement can be agreed.

In the County Court, the issue of proceedings involves the solicitor sending or taking a summons, a court form and particulars of claim (which sets out the details of the case against the defendant) and a fee to the County Court. The court will enter an action number on the summons after sealing it with the court seal.

The solicitor may also file the expert's report at court – in particular a medical report and the calculation of special damages (by accountants) in a personal injury case. The summons, particulars of claim (and, if appropriate, medical report and the calculation of special damages) must then be *served* on the defendant.

In the High Court, the solicitor will prepare a *writ* with a *statement of claim*. The writ is a particular form to be used to start cases in the High Court. The statement of claim simply sets out what the plaintiff's claim is, i.e. it performs the same function that the particulars of claim does in the County Court. When the writ is issued by the court, it will be sealed and an action number will be entered on the top right-hand side. The writ is then served on the defendant (again an expert's report may be included at this stage). Sometimes the writ is served alone and the statement of claim shortly afterwards. In personal injury cases, medical reports and calculation of special damages must be included with the statement of claim.

The action number set out on the summons or the writ is a useful reference number for the expert to quote when sending further correspondence or reports to the solicitors.

EXCHANGE OF PLEADINGS

The exchange of pleadings involves the parties sending each other the court documents that they have drawn up. It enables the defendant to see the case against them and the plaintiff to see what the defendant's defence is.

Pleadings are legally drafted documents which set out what happened and what the parties want – they are the arguments put forward by the parties. The object of pleadings is to define the issues between the parties on which the parties require the court to adjudicate. They give each party notice of the issues to be contested and the facts that will be raised. The summons and the writ are the first formal court documents in the "pleadings".

After service of the summons or writ, there are further pleadings. Firstly, the defendant puts in a **defence** and, if appropriate, a

counterclaim. (A counterclaim is a pleading in which the defendant alleges that the plaintiff's conduct has caused the defendant loss and damage.) Secondly, the plaintiff may file a reply to the defence and, if appropriate, a defence to counterclaim.

In the High Court, the "close of pleadings" occurs 14 days after service of a reply or, if there is no reply, after service of the defence and counterclaim. If neither a reply nor a defence to counterclaim is served, the close of pleadings occurs 14 days after service of the defence. In the County Court, the close of pleadings occurs 14 days after the service of the defence or 28 days after the service of a defence and counterclaim. The close of pleadings is a significant time in terms of the procedural time limits that are now in place to regulate the speed of the litigation.

Further and Better Particulars

Either party may request more details about the case from the opposing party. Experts can help the solicitors in deciding what to ask.

DISCOVERY/DISCLOSURE AND INSPECTION OF EVIDENCE

The purpose of discovery and inspection of evidence is to avoid surprise evidence at trial. There can be no trial by ambush. Each party is entitled to see the evidence that the other party will be using at the trial.

Discovery involves the disclosure by one party to the other of the *existence* of all relevant documents which each party has in its custody, possession or control. This is done by way of a list of documents. This will then be followed by the *inspection* by the other party's solicitor of those documents. Examples are letters, statements and expert reports which are not privileged, such as the expert's final report which is to be be used at trial. If both parties can see the evidence, it may help the parties to reach a settlement without the need for a trial.

Sometimes discovery in the High Court or the County Court is automatic. There are automatic directions which are a list of rules designed to set out necessary steps for the parties to undertake before trial. If discovery is not automatic, then the plaintiff's solicitor will take out a summons for directions, which means the court will state when discovery and inspection should take place.

The Impact of Discovery on Experts' Reports

Discovery is the seeing of each party's evidence, including experts' reports, by the other party.

If an expert's report has already been served on the other side, for example with the particulars of claim (in the County Court) or with the statement of claim (in the High Court), there will be no further impact made by discovery/disclosure. However, if the expert's report has not already been disclosed, there are some important rules that apply on disclosure.

1. Communications between the solicitor and a third party (e.g. an expert witness or a witness as to fact) are privileged from inspection if they came into existence for the purpose of pending litigation. Thus witness statements (witness as to fact) and unfavourable expert reports, or earlier versions of an expert's report, which are not going to be relied on as evidence at trial do not have to be revealed.

2. However, the general rule is that trials cannot be conducted by ambush and so, if a party *does intend to rely* at trial on the evidence of a witness as to fact or an expert's report, then the substance of that evidence must be disclosed in a written form to the other party within a specified period.

A limit may be placed on the number of experts that may be called by each party. The experts' reports are usually exchanged simultaneously. It may also be directed or, if not directed, arranged between the parties that a meeting "without prejudice" takes place between experts to try to agree their reports if possible and, if not, to identify the areas where their evidence is in issue. (See Meetings with Other Experts in Chapter 2.) The effect of a without prejudice meeting is that, without prejudging the issues, each party can discuss the case frankly while, if a settlement is not reached, the conversations or admissions made cannot be repeated at trial.

It is often possible at this stage for the parties to see their relative strengths and weaknesses more clearly and to agree a settlement. If the case proceeds to trial, the experts whose reports have been disclosed can be called to give evidence. An expert should then be able to focus on the strengths of his/her opinion and to seek to persuade the judge that his/her independent expert opinion is to be preferred to that of the other expert.

What the Woolf Report Says about Solicitors' Instructions and Experts' Draft Reports

Lord Woolf, in his report into the civil justice system *Access to Justice*, made recommendations on the use of expert evidence.

In Chapter 13, paragraphs 31-33, the report accepted that it was unrealistic to insist that experts' draft reports were disclosed. The position is therefore the same as before, i.e. only the report to be relied on at trial must be disclosed.

However, it was stated that the *instructions* given by solicitors to experts should be disclosable. It recommended that expert evidence should not be admissible (allowed) at trial unless *written instructions* (including letters subsequent upon original instructions) and a note of any *oral instructions* are included as an annex to the expert's report.

39

It is regarded as essential that, where there are diverging opinions in two experts' reports, the parties and the judge should know the basis on which the experts have been instructed. Ideally, the experts should receive joint or agreed instructions, as this makes it easier to compare the reports.

See Appendix 3 for full wording of the relevant paragraphs of the Woolf Report.

Work with the Lawyers during Discovery

It may be that after discovery the expert witness alters his or her opinion and they should, of course, communicate this to their instructing solicitors. Equally, it is very important that any new materials are passed on to the expert by the solicitors. A further report may be needed.

An expert witness will also often be asked to provide comments on the expert report disclosed by the other party.

SETTLEMENT

This is where the two parties to a dispute reach an agreement without the need for the case to proceed to a court hearing or further steps in the litigation process. The vast majority (about 96%) of civil cases settle before trial. It is in the interests of both parties to reach a settlement rather than to have to spend time and money on a trial. Sometimes the matter may be settled prior to litigation starting as a result of the preliminary report of the expert witness.

There are many other opportunities to reach a settlement as the litigation progresses. It is often possible to settle cases after disclosure of all the evidence. Each side can then assess the relative strengths and weaknesses of their case. The expert's role in reaching settlement can be crucial. An expert's report which identifies all the strengths of a case and is able to deal effectively with any areas of weakness is an essential tool in reaching settlement.

Settlement can take place at any time. It can even take place at the door of the court or during the trial.

Any "without prejudice" documents produced with a view to settlement are protected by privilege. In the event of negotiations being unsuccessful, these documents cannot be referred to at trial. (See details of this in Chapter 2.)

FIXING THE DATE FOR THE TRIAL

Fixing the trial date is called "setting down" for trial. The date will be agreed between the court official in charge and the solicitors. Solicitors notify the court that they want a trial date and will be given an actual date or likely date for the trial. Solicitors can take into account the availability of barristers and also expert witnesses. It is worthwhile for the expert witness to let the solicitor have a list of dates to be avoided if possible.

PROCEDURE OF A CIVIL TRIAL

1. The plaintiff's advocate makes an opening speech. He or she explains the facts to the judge and sets out the issues in dispute.

2. In rare cases, the defence may make an opening speech.

3. The plaintiff's witnesses give evidence. Each witness will be examined-in-chief by the plaintiff's lawyer and then cross-examined by the defendant's lawyer. The witness may be re-examined by the plaintiff's lawyer if anything new has come up in the cross-examination which requires clarification.

4. The defendant's witnesses give evidence, in the same way as the plaintiff's witnesses do.

5. Closing speeches: the defendant's lawyer goes first, followed by the plaintiff's lawyer.

Note that exchange of witness of fact statements and expert reports means that each party will know in advance what oral evidence the witnesses will give. Note also that it is the evidence given in the witness box which the judge takes into account when reaching a decision.

EVIDENCE IN CIVIL TRIALS

Evidence in civil trials, like that in criminal trials, can be divided into three categories: documentary evidence, real evidence and witness evidence.

Documentary evidence includes photographs, video recordings and tape recordings, as well as documents (such as letters, internal memoranda, hospital notes) made by the parties themselves during the period which is the focus of the action.

Real evidence is any material object produced to the court for inspection. This may include anything from a blood coated dagger in a trial of trespass to the person, to the automatic recording of radar traces showing the position of a ship in an Admiralty action. Confusingly, photographs, video recordings and tape recordings may be both "documents" and real evidence.

With regard to witnesses, once again there are three types: witnesses of fact, expert witnesses and professional witnesses.

WITNESSES OF FACT

A witness of fact in a civil trial is someone who is called to give evidence in a case about what happened. They are there to recall what they saw or heard. They are not generally allowed to give opinion evidence. Contrast this with an expert witness who may give both factual *and* opinion evidence.

There are many kinds of witnesses as to fact in civil cases, such as a witness who saw a car accident in which the plaintiff was injured; a witness who recalls the medical advice given to a patient who has a claim for professional negligence; and a witness who recorded the results of a scientific experiment.

A witness as to fact will generally give oral evidence at trial. This is because oral evidence is deemed to be the best form of evidence as it can be tested under cross-examination.

Witnesses giving oral evidence in the witness box may refresh their memory from any contemporaneous notes they may have kept. Contemporaneous notes are records completed while the facts were still fresh in the witness's mind. Such a contemporaneous note is part of the oral evidence and may be read out by the witness. The other party has the right to request and inspect such notes. Frequently, the contemporaneous notes will comprise the witness's statement.

Examples of such notes are a police officer's notebook, a scrap of paper on which a passer-by has written down the registration number of a car involved in an accident, records of scientific experiments, records of an audit carried out by accountants, medical records, etc.

Where experts are to give factual evidence, it is important for them to keep accurate and full notes. The following information is important:

- Dates, time, location.

- Who was present (patient, client, researchers).

- Examinations/experiments and findings.

- Details of observed facts and, if an expert, his/her opinion on the facts.

- Details of conversations/advice given.

Witness Statements in Civil Trials

Witnesses of fact write statements, not reports. A statement will usually be written some time after the events it records. It will usually be written at the prompting of a solicitor. The purpose of such a statement is to set out in writing the details of a particular event or series or events.

The statement itself will not normally be evidence at the trial. The evidence will come from the mouth of the witness in the witness box. However, there will be times when a statement will "stand as evidence" and will take the place of examination in chief (questions asked by the lawyer of the party who calls the witness). Further, if the statement is not controversial and the other side does not wish to cross-examine the witness about it, the statement may be read out in court without the necessity of the witness attending.

A witness statement is always available for the witness to refresh his or her memory before going into the witness box to give evidence. If the witness has contemporaneous notes, then those can be taken into the witness box.

The oral evidence to be given by the witness will be known in advance since there is a duty to exchange witness statements in advance of the trial.

EXPERT WITNESSES

An expert witness may give evidence of both fact and opinion.

Facts fall into two different categories. Firstly, there are facts that experts have observed for themselves, for example the crack in the floor of a building, an X-ray, or the accounts of one of the parties.

Secondly, there are facts that an expert has been told by someone else, for example the date on which a floor of a building was completed, the amount of pain being suffered by a patient, or the reason why certain items in the accounts have been described as extraordinary items. This category will include facts that have been reported to an expert by a member of his/her team of researchers or auditors (these people will often be called as witnesses too).

Experts must take great care to identify the source of the facts on which they base their expert opinion. Facts which an expert has observed first-hand will usually be given greater weight than facts that the expert has been told by another person. The veracity of facts reported to an expert by another person may be tested at trial by the cross-examination of the person who supplied those facts to the expert. For example, a plaintiff in a personal injury case may be cross-examined about whether he really was suffering from the level of pain he told his expert surgeon he was suffering from. It may be suggested in cross-examination that the plaintiff was exaggerating his condition or simply lying.

Expert opinion evidence is admissible in court on matters not within the common knowledge of the court. It can be based upon experiment, experience, research or the work of others. Experts are entitled to give such opinion evidence because of their qualifications and experience in their field of expertise.

It has already been seen that any expert's report which is to be relied upon at trial must be disclosed to the other party well before the trial. If the experts on both sides agree with one another, their reports may be read at trial without the need for either of them to attend.

In more complicated cases, the experts may have a "without prejudice" meeting prior to trial. A without prejudice meeting is a meeting at which anything said by the parties cannot be used to prejudge the issues at trial. This is to promote frank discussion between the parties. The aim of this meeting will be to iron out differences and to identify those issues on which agreement cannot be reached. At trial, cross-examination will focus on these areas of disagreement.

Opinion on Liability and Quantum

In most civil cases, the judge will make the decision on liability and quantum. However, the judge will be helped by hearing the opinion of expert witnesses. For example, a forensic accountant may be asked to assess the amount of money a plaintiff has lost by reason of injuries the plaintiff sustained in a road traffic accident.

PROFESSIONAL WITNESSES

Most professional witnesses give evidence as a result of seeing or doing something in the course of their everyday job. Giving evidence will be a part of their job. Good examples of professional witnesses are police officers and police surgeons. Professional witnesses give mainly factual evidence but can give opinion evidence based on their qualifications and experience. Their evidence is given in the form of a statement and not a report. This statement may be read out in court without the need for them to give oral evidence. However, the other party may ask for them to be called to give evidence and to be cross-examined.

Professional witnesses are classified separately from expert witnesses for the purpose of establishing the relevant rate of payment by the Legal Aid Board.

WITNESS ATTENDANCE

It is usual for solicitors to ask their own client's witnesses whether they will attend court voluntarily or not. If a witness refuses to reply to the solicitor's enquiry or indicates that they will not attend voluntarily, then the solicitor will get the court to make an order that the witness attends. A witness will be served in the High Court or in the County Court with a subpoena or a witness summons. If a witness fails to attend after having been served with a subpoena or a witness summons, they may be arrested and fined and/or imprisoned. Certain categories of witnesses (such as police officers) will often ask the solicitor to arrange for them to be served with a witness summons/subpoena because they need such a document in order to prove to their employer that they are required to have time off work to attend a civil trial!

Chapter 2

THE ROLE OF THE EXPERT WITNESS

SUMMARY

- The need for expert witnesses ●
- The differences between lawyers and expert witnesses ●
- What lawyers require from experts ●
- Taking instructions from lawyers ●
- Meetings with other experts ●
- Professional negligence and breach of contract ●

THE NEED FOR EXPERT WITNESSES

Expert witnesses are individuals with qualifications and experience which enable them to give opinions on the facts of cases within their specialist field. They are independent of the case although often paid by one of the parties. Their role is to help the lawyers and court to understand technical matters in the case and assist in advising on the strength of the case. Their evidence will be in two forms, a written report and oral evidence given in the witness box.

The functions of an expert can be classified as follows:

1. To provide a *preliminary report* to help the solicitor decide whether the solicitor's client has a case and, if so, what the strengths and weaknesses are. (See Chapter 1.)

2. To provide a *final report* for the court. (See Chapter 3.)

3. To help lawyers in drafting legal documents needed for the court and in negotiating a settlement.

4. To comment on other experts' findings at all stages in the proceedings.

5. To give oral evidence at trial from the witness box.

The expert's role is similar whichever of the above functions he or she is performing and is set out below. The expert will spend a lot of time working with the party's lawyers but is also responsible for providing an independent report for the court.

THE ROLE OF THE EXPERT WITNESS: TO GIVE OPINION EVIDENCE

The role of the expert witness is commonly misunderstood or confused with the role of the lawyers.

An expert witness is needed to give clear, independent opinion evidence on the subject within his or her field. This field is defined by reference to the expert's qualifications and experience. An expert should not give opinion evidence outside his or her field of expertise and should not accept the role in cases outside their expertise.

An expert's role is thus as an educator, in the first instance to assist the lawyers in the preparation of the case which includes doing a report for court and secondly, if the case goes to court, to assist the judge to reach a fair decision, with the aid of the report.

Where legal proceedings are in progress, expert advisers will often be retained separately by each party. However, experts are not hired guns. Their role is not to win the case. The lawyers are paid to do that. The lawyers are the advocates who represent their clients' arguments, the expert is a witness giving *evidence* of his or her opinion, based on his or her knowledge. Experts must avoid biased, exaggerated evidence.

Expert witness evidence is very important. It must be based on a sound foundation of *facts* which have been properly and vigorously investigated. Acquiring these facts may involve such activities as examining a patient, asking a patient questions, conducting an experiment or visiting the site of a building which has structural problems. No stone should be left unturned. Experts should always be prepared to explain why they reached their expert opinion given a certain set of facts.

THE ROLE OF THE LAWYER: TO REPRESENT THE PARTY

Lawyers represent their client's case in court. They are not neutral or objective but partisan. They are paid to win. The lawyers have to do the best they can with the available evidence. They have a discretion in deciding which evidence to use and how to present it and will marshal it in a way that is most favourable to their client's case. However, lawyers must not knowingly present false evidence and have a duty not to positively mislead the court. For example, they must not knowingly allow a witness to tell lies in the witness box.

The lawyers *do not give evidence* – they are not witnesses. Their role is to argue and seek to persuade the judge to decide in favour of their client.

DIFFERENCES BETWEEN AN EXPERT WITNESS AND A LAWYER

Expert Witness	Lawyer
Independent	Partisan
Neutral	Biased
Knows about field not law	Knows about law, not field
Witness	Advocate
Gives evidence	Represents the client
Never argues	Argues
Assists the judge	Persuades the judge
Not a hired gun	A hired gun

WHAT THE INSTRUCTING LAWYERS REQUIRE FROM AN EXPERT

It is important to understand what the lawyers require.

When an expert witness is to be engaged, the lawyers will want to make sure that the expert is the right person for the case. In an initial meeting or telephone call with the lawyers, an expert should expect to be asked probing questions, for example about qualifications and experience or whether the expert has had previous court experience. The lawyers will listen to the responses and note the level of confidence, the clarity of expression and the expert's overall honesty and integrity.

An expert who is defensive, confused or verbose is likely to be avoided by lawyers.

Do not be intimidated by a lack of previous court experience. It is expertise in a particular field that is important.

An expert may come under pressure from the solicitors or barristers to modify or change their opinion to help the lawyers to win the case. However, the expert should bear in mind the words of Lord Wilberforce in *Whitehouse v Jordan* ([1981] 1 WLR 246 at page 256):

"It is necessary that expert evidence presented to the court should be, and should be seen to be, the independent product of the expert, uninfluenced as to form or content by the exigences of litigation. To the extent that it is not, the evidence is likely to be not only incorrect but self-defeating."

Remember that the expert's professional credibility is on the line if the lawyer persuades him or her to exaggerate the true position in terms of their expert opinion.

The lawyers who have instructed you may persuade you to paint a very rosy picture in your report and also in court. Be careful to

51

answer questions truthfully and provide a reasoned basis for your opinion.

TAKING INSTRUCTIONS: WHAT THE EXPERT NEEDS TO KNOW

- Are you the right expert for the job? Be clear on what the lawyer needs expertise in. A General Practitioner should not profess to be an expert in open heart surgery!

- What are the deadlines/time limits for writing a report?

- How much will you be paid (see Chapter 5 on fees)?

- What are the terms and conditions for you providing your expert service (see Chapter 3)?

- Have proceedings started yet? Has the writ or summons been issued (see Chapter 1)?

- Do the lawyers want a preliminary report (to see if there is a case for the plaintiff to bring), a final report or both?

- If proceedings have started, at what stage are they?

- Are there any court documents prepared by the lawyers? For example the particulars of claim or the statement of claim, the defence/counterclaim. These can be very helpful as they set out the main issues in the case.

- Are there any witness statements? Can you see them?

- Are there any reports from experts instructed by other parties to the proceedings? Can you see them?

- Are there any other experts instructed by the solicitor instructing you? What are their areas of expertise? What are their findings and opinions?

● Do you have copies of all essential documents, photographs, witness statements, diagrams, etc.?

● What do the lawyers want you to do – to look at liability or quantum (see Chapter 1, page 46)?

● Do you need permission/consent to visit a site or examine a patient and have the lawyers obtained this consent?

Do not be afraid to ask the lawyers if you do not understand what you are being asked to do.

Be proactive in getting detailed instructions as you go along. Help to educate the lawyers as to what the issues are. In complex technical areas, the expert is more likely to be able to see what the issues are than the lawyers.

Duty of Confidentiality to Instructing Solicitor's Client

The expert witness is instructed and paid by the solicitors, not the client. The contract is between the solicitors and the expert. However, communications between the expert and the solicitor cannot be disclosed without the *consent* of the solicitor's client. Expert reports likewise cannot be disclosed to the other side unless the solicitor's client gives consent. The rules on disclosure of reports have already been discussed in detail in Chapter 1.

How Legal Professional Privilege Affects the Expert Witness

Communications between solicitors and their client, and communications between an expert witness and instructing solicitors are protected or privileged from being seen by anyone but the instructing solicitors and the client. This protection exists so long as what the expert is saying or writing is done for the purpose of giving advice in litigation and it comes into existence after litigation was contemplated or commenced. However, once it has been decided that the expert witness's report is to be used as evidence at trial, the contents of this report must be revealed or disclosed to the other side. This is known as discovery. An expert witness should ensure that anything which is within their report which they wish to remain confidential is drawn to the attention of the lawyers and is thus not revealed at disclosure.

Any matter which is not disclosed cannot later be relied on at court during the trial.

COACHING

Solicitors or Barristers Cannot Coach Witnesses

Expert witnesses are an important resource for lawyers. Cases can be won or lost on the strength of the expert's opinion evidence. However, lawyers are bound by their own professional rules *not* to coach witnesses, that is they cannot tell witnesses what they ought to say.

Can Experts Coach Lawyers?

Yes, they can and should. One of the most important roles of an expert witness is to work with the lawyers to help to clarify and explain complex technical areas. Experts can also help the barrister to ask them the right questions during the trial and also to put the right questions to the experts called for the other party at trial.

MEETINGS WITH OTHER EXPERTS

The Purpose of Meetings Between Experts

The purpose of a "without prejudice" meeting between experts is twofold. Firstly to discuss technical matters within their expertise and secondly to discuss their respective opinions on these technical matters. It is important for expert witnesses to have a frank discussion of the strengths and weaknesses of the case. These meetings enable the experts to pool the relevant technical information, to highlight areas where further investigation is required and prevent significant matters being overlooked. A greater understanding of the issues can be acquired as well as a greater understanding of the reasons for the other expert's opinion. If the reports have not yet been written, this will help the experts to write shorter, clearer and more relevant reports.

The experts must record, and may wish to produce a joint statement of, matters that are agreed and those that are still in dispute. Such agreements between the experts are not legally binding; they are without prejudice and cannot be used at any subsequent trial.

There are two types of meetings, those ordered by the court and those agreed between the parties. Below is a summary of the main differences between these meetings.

Court Orders for Meetings Prior to Trial

In civil proceedings the court may *order* a "without prejudice" meeting. This means that what is said or agreed between experts cannot be used in evidence at the subsequent trial. The court will define the object of the meeting and give the experts authority to discuss those matters.

An expert does not have the power to reach a binding agreement with another expert during these meetings, since the expert does not represent the party but is an independent witness.

Lawyers and the parties may not be present during court ordered "without prejudice" meetings. However, the lawyers can negotiate an agreement between the parties after such meetings.

Once a trial has started, the court cannot order a meeting of experts, although the parties can agree meetings.

Meeting *Agreed* Between the Parties

The parties may *agree* to a "without prejudice" meeting of experts at any time before or during the trial. The parties themselves define the object of such a meeting and the lawyers and the parties may be present. The experts can be given varying degrees of authority from being allowed to settle nothing to reaching agreement, although only after consulting the lawyers. The expert must be clear on what the main issues in dispute are and if in doubt the meeting should be adjourned to consult the party's solicitor.

Preparation for a meeting with other experts is very important. The lawyers can help with identifying the main issues. It is helpful if the lawyers draft a list of questions which the experts should answer. The experts should draw up a joint document at the end of the meeting. This will list each issue that the experts consider important. Both experts will indicate under these headings areas of agreement or disagreement and give their reasons.

Use of Without Prejudice Documents

"Without prejudice" means that information can be frankly exchanged without "prejudging" the issue with a view to promoting a settlement. Comments or admissions made cannot later be used at the trial if the parties fail to reach a settlement. Letters or communications which are made "without prejudice" are privileged and protected from disclosure at trial. In addition, evidence cannot be given of oral communications which took place "without prejudice". If frank discussions – oral or written – take place, where admissions are made and a settlement is not reached, these admissions and/or discussions will not be admissible at trial.

However, this rule is only applied where the oral or written communication was made with the *purpose of reaching settlement of a dispute.*

The presence or absence of the words "without prejudice" is not in itself conclusive. Merely to put "without prejudice" on correspondence will not automatically provide protection from disclosure. It will only do so if the purpose of the correspondence or conversation was to settle the dispute.

It is, however, prudent to agree that a meeting to negotiate a settlement is "without prejudice". It is also sensible to put "without prejudice" on top of any correspondence written with a view to helping to achieve settlement.

What the Woolf Report Says about Expert Meetings Post-October 1998

In Chapter 13, paragraphs 42-51 of his 1996 report *Access to Justice*, Lord Woolf suggests an increased use of experts' meetings to allow settlement of disputes without the need for an expensive court trial. However, he argues that the present arrangements for meetings of expert witnesses hinder their ability to meet and agree issues. He cites some reservations with the present system: "Meetings can be futile because the experts are instructed not to agree anything; or alternatively are told that any points of agreement must be referred back to their instructing lawyers for ratification."

To avoid this problem, Lord Woolf suggests that it should be unprofessional conduct for an expert to be given, or to accept, instructions not to reach agreement.

Lord Woolf makes several other recommendations about the organisation of experts' meetings, all designed to narrow down the issues to enable settlement or a shorter trial.

1. Preparation for Meeting

Experts to prepare an agreed chronology and statement of facts, with a summary of important or disputed points. It would be helpful to do this as soon as possible after submission of the defence and thus help to define the scope of the expert's report, before the report is written. If, however, the first meeting takes place after the exchange of expert reports, it can still provide a helpful guideline for discussion.

2. Preparation of an Agenda for the Meeting

Lord Woolf suggests that in complex cases it is the court who should set the agenda. The purpose is to narrow the issues that are in dispute. It is desirable that, in the absence of the court setting an agenda, the experts should have an agreed agenda. If each expert has their own agenda then there is a tendency for the meeting to end up being little more than an opportunity for the experts to flex their muscles and argue their own corner.

The agenda should be prepared at least a week before the meeting and should aim to list the areas of dispute. Facts and opinions of both experts in relation to these areas should be highlighted.

3. Conduct of the Meetings

Lord Woolf would like meetings between experts to be in private without the lawyers being present. He accepts that there are some circumstances in which this will not be appropriate. He suggests that when the court directs a meeting, the parties should have to make an application for the lawyers to be present. When the lawyers do attend, they should be present simply as observers and should not participate in the discussions or agreement.

These suggestions will greatly increase the role and responsibility of experts at meetings. The expert must be well prepared and flexible in approach. He or she must listen carefully to the facts, assumptions and opinions put forward by the other expert and see if there is scope for agreement on any of the issues. The expert should note carefully the times, dates and details of these meetings.

4. At the End of the Meeting

Lord Woolf recommends that at the end of the meeting the experts produce for the court a written list of agreed matters of professional opinion and issues still in dispute. It is then for the parties and their lawyers to consider the effect of any agreement or disagreement on the future conduct of the case. Experts must note agreed and disagreed matters.

These recommendations, though not yet law, highlight the importance of proper preparation and planning for experts' meetings. It is suggested that it is good practice to adopt many of the recommendations made by Lord Woolf.

See Appendix 3 for the full text of the relevant paragraphs of the Woolf Report.

PROFESSIONAL NEGLIGENCE AND BREACH OF CONTRACT

Expert witnesses must appreciate the responsibility they have for their own evidence. An expert witness is responsible for carrying out a full and thorough investigation into the facts. The lawyers will often rely on the expert to study documents, and carry out experiments and research to find out all the available information.

The evidence an expert presents in a report or in court is their evidence, not the lawyers'. If the expert has carried out insufficient investigations, or has become too partisan in their opinion, he or she may later be found to be in breach of contract or negligent. The main pitfalls for experts are:

- Inadequate instructions taken from solicitor – the instructions do not point out all the issues. However, the expert is paid to point out all the issues and so should look beyond the instructions given.

- Failure to give independent/impartial advice. The expert's opinion becomes distorted under pressure from the lawyers. Remember, it is the *expert's* opinion evidence not the lawyer's. An expert can be sued for giving an opinion that no reasonable expert in that field of expertise could come to. *The expert must give bona fide independent expert opinion.*

- Failure of communication between the solicitor's client and the expert. Take full statements in writing from the client.

- Failure to agree in writing what service the expert is providing for the instructing solicitors. There will often be a gap between the service given and the service expected. The expert should be clear as to what (s)he is giving expert advice on and what the purpose of this advice is.

- Breach of confidentiality by expert or defamation of someone in the report.

- Technical errors. An example is an expert who was found to be negligent because he grossly over-valued the potential damages the plaintiff would get awarded at trial. The plaintiff, on the basis of this information, did not accept an early payment into court by the defendant. Later the plaintiff was awarded damages of significantly less. (A payment into court is where one party gives money to the court to be given to the other party. The other party can withdraw that money and end the case. If they do not, then they are liable for all the legal costs of the case from then on if the judge orders a lesser sum to be paid at the trial.)

- Failure to acknowledge other possibilities. Consider if it is appropriate to say "If A happened, then .....; if B, then .....". This will show an awareness of different factors and also indicate an unwillingness to conceal information.

How to Avoid Claims of Professional Negligence/Breach of Contract

1. The expert must be able to prove that (s)he did a good job and exercised reasonable care and skill to avoid a successful claim of professional negligence. The expert must keep good notes of what (s)he did.

2. Keep up to date through training/research, etc.

3. Be clear in the advice given and keep the lawyers informed.

4. Ask for more information and indicate if you have insufficient factual evidence on which to base an opinion.

Key Contents of Good Notes

- Basic information such as dates, time, location.

- Who else was present, e.g. other employees, a patient, the solicitor's client, a police officer.

- If consent was to be obtained, how was this done?

- What was the purpose of an examination, site visit or experiment?

- The findings of the examination or investigation.

- Detailed observation of *facts* and *opinions*.

- Details of any follow-up inspection or examination.

It is important to note that it may be several years before you personally, or your company, are sued for negligence. You *must* be able to verify what actually happened and why.

Consider a consultant gynaecologist who delivers hundreds of babies each year. Three years after the delivery of a particular child, he/she has a claim of professional negligence brought against him/her. The court will not be impressed with "memory" only. In cross-examination that consultant will be pulled to pieces unless there is some concrete evidence of what actually happened.

Keep your notes for at least six years (as breach of contract cases can be brought for up to six years after the breach is discovered. Negligence cases can be brought up to three years after the negligent act).

Professional Indemnity Insurance

No matter how careful or experienced an expert is in a field, it is possible to make mistakes. It is imperative to have professional indemnity insurance. These insurance policies not only pay damages but can also help with payment of the legal costs of any investigation, settlement or defence work.

Professional indemnity insurers have access to expert lawyers and loss adjusters to give expert witnesses the best possible defence.

Chapter 3

WRITING REPORTS

SUMMARY

- The purpose of a report
- How the report will be used in court
- Agreeing terms and conditions
- How to write an excellent report
- The content of the report
- The presentation of the report
- The writing process

WHAT IS THE PURPOSE OF A REPORT?

A report is written by an expert witness to help the lawyers in the preparation of the case and also to help the court to reach a decision. The report is for people who are not experts in the specialist field that the report is about. The report must contain written details of all the facts which the expert has relied on to reach his or her opinion, which should be a reasoned analysis of the strengths and weaknesses of the case. The expert should try as far as possible to anticipate all the possible arguments that may be put forward by the other party's expert. These arguments should be addressed and any weaknesses pointed out. The expert should aim to persuade the judge/jury that his/her expert opinion is to be preferred to the other expert's opinion as it has more strengths.

The facts and opinion should be tailored to address the key issues in the case that the lawyers will have to establish. For example, in a professional negligence claim, the issues are 1) that the professional person was acting in a situation where a duty of care to the client was owed; 2) that there was a breach of this duty, i.e. no reasonable professional person would have acted in that way; and 3) that the breach caused the damage/injury.

Expert witnesses may be asked to write preliminary reports. These are reports written primarily to help the solicitors and their clients decide if the plaintiff has a worthwhile case to commence an action against an individual or company. More often, experts are asked to write final reports as the litigation has already started. These reports form the basis for negotiating settlements or are for use at the trial.

HOW THE REPORT WILL BE USED IN COURT

At trial, the expert may or may not be called to give oral evidence and be cross-examined in the witness box.

In criminal trials, the report may be in the form of a section 9 statement. This means that it has been served on the other party and the other party does not object to it being read in court instead of calling the witness to give oral evidence. If the other party objects to the section 9 statement, then the witness will have to give oral evidence and be cross-examined.

There is also an opportunity in civil trials for the parties to agree that the expert's report can be used as evidence without calling the expert to give oral evidence.

The judge in civil cases, and the judge and jury in criminal cases, will have a copy of the report if it is admissible without the need to call the witness, whether or not the expert is called to give oral evidence. Where the witness is giving oral evidence, it makes it easier for them to follow the evidence. The expert witness should use the report to help explain points to the judge and/or jury.

AGREE TERMS AND CONDITIONS BEFORE WRITING THE REPORT

The contract for services is between the expert witness and the instructing solicitors. It is not between the solicitors' client and the expert witness. If the solicitors are not paid by the client, they are still obliged to pay the expert witness.

You should have a standard pro forma letter to send out on receiving instructions, setting out your terms and conditions. The following matters should be covered:

1. *Set out what you understand are the services you are expected to perform.*

   Preparation of preliminary and/or final report, attendance at meetings, attendance at conference with counsel, attendance at court, etc. It is important to be clear on this. A gap between what you think you are to do and what the solicitors think they have asked you to do can often give rise to negligence claims against the expert witness.

2. *Set out the obligations of the instructing solicitors.*

   Detail all the evidence and documents you wish the solicitor to provide you with – the plaintiff's statement, all medical reports relating to the plaintiff, the plaintiff's statement of claim, the defence and counterclaim, reports of other experts, advice from counsel, all relevant documents, witness statements, etc.

3. *Set out the obligations that you have as the expert.*

   That you will use reasonable skill and care in the performance of instructions given to you, preserve the confidentiality of information/documents/correspondence relating to the case.

4. *Fees.*

   Indicate that these will be based on the amount of time involved and the degree of skill or responsibility required. Deal with privately funded cases separately from legally aid cases.

See Appendix 1 for a specimen pro forma on terms and conditions.

It is very important that the issue of fees is addressed at this stage. As only about 4% of cases actually get to court (the rest being settled beforehand), most experts invoice the solicitors after the report has been written. Even if the case is to go to court, a preliminary invoice for the writing of the report should be sent.

The payment of experts' fees is dealt with fully in Chapter 5.

WRITING AN EXCELLENT EXPERT REPORT

Expert evidence in court takes two forms: the expert's written report and their oral evidence. However, as some 96% of civil cases settle without going to court, the majority of cases are settled on the basis of the written evidence in the form of the expert's report.

An excellent report can influence the client, the solicitors who instruct you, the barristers giving advice to your party, and the other party's expert, solicitors and barristers. If the case goes to court, the report must be able to influence the person who decides the case – the judge, the jury or the magistrates.

You are completely in control of the written evidence in your report. If you are called to give oral evidence at court, you will gain a lot of confidence by having an excellent report to which you can refer to help explain the case and your opinion. A good report often forms the core document in the case.

The purpose of a report is to provide *information* for the parties to the case and, if the case goes to court, for the judge. The information must be set out in a succinct, clear, easy to read style.

Remember that the report is to be used by people who are not experts in your field. Imagine the judge using your report as a pair of spectacles to look at the evidence so it comes into sharp focus.

Report writing is a two stage process: firstly gathering factual information by interviewing witnesses, visiting the scene, carrying out detailed research and investigations, etc. and secondly coming to your expert opinion on those facts.

Get Clear Instructions for Writing Your Report

Make sure the instructions you receive from the lawyers are as clear as possible and do not make any assumptions. Before you start your investigations and research, find out what you are supposed to be doing. As the expert, you may have a clearer idea of what the issues are than the solicitors have. Discuss the issues with the solicitors until you are both happy with what you are supposed to be looking at. Good instructions will ensure you write an excellent report.

Solicitors may not give you the instructions you need. They may simply send you a letter saying "Please do a report" without telling you what the case is about.

Ask the solicitors for what you need. You may be able to do this in simple cases by sending them a pro forma letter which asks who the parties are, what the facts are, how long you have to write the report, the amount you will be paid per hour/per report. In criminal cases, ask what the charge is and what the defence is. In civil cases, ask why one party is suing another. In more complex cases you will need to speak to the solicitors on a more regular basis. If you do not understand what you are supposed to be doing or what the issues are, then do not be afraid to ask until you do understand. Be proactive, remember you are the expert – you know what you need, the lawyers may not. You also need to be clear about fees from the outset (see Chapter 5 and pro forma letter in Appendix 1).

What is the Purpose of this Particular Report?

You may be doing a preliminary report, that is a report to be used by solicitors to decide if their client has a case worth pursuing. You may be doing a report to assist a barrister draft the formal court documents (pleadings) stating what the case is about.

You may be doing a final report which will be used to settle the case or used at court. Consider the different needs of different readers. You may want to modify the report according to its purpose.

In both civil and criminal cases, you only have to disclose to the other party to the litigation the report which will be relied on at trial; earlier versions need not be disclosed. (See Chapter 1 on disclosure.)

Investigation of Facts

Make a proper detailed investigation of the facts. Full investigation and research are essential. You may discover facts by observation or from documents by yourself or with the help of others. Do not make any assumptions. Note carefully the sources of your facts, you will need to include these in the report.

Keep Fully Informed

To write an excellent report, you need to be fully informed of all aspects of the case. You need to have access to all the facts on which you are to base your expert opinion. You should ask the lawyers to provide you with all the documentation. You may be a better judge of what is and is not relevant to the issue upon which you are giving your expert opinion. As the case develops, check with the lawyers to make sure they have given you any additional documentation. If you need to go back to the witnesses to get further details, do not be afraid to do so.

Know Who Will Read the Report

The expert's report will be read by the parties, the parties' lawyers and, most importantly, by the decision maker – the judge (and jury in Crown Court criminal trials) or magistrates. The report must be capable of being understood by all these people who are not experts in the field.

The report must be easy for the reader to understand. The judge will be a busy person who may not be at all familiar with the specialist/ technical area that you are writing about. Aim to avoid jargon and set out the facts and your opinion in an interesting and easily understood way. Explain any technical terms clearly. Make the report as accessible as you can with a detailed contents page indicating where the facts of the case are set out, where the opinion can be found and where your conclusion is.

What Does the Reader Need to Know?

You cannot write a report for use in legal proceedings in the same way that you write a document to be read by another professional in your field. A report which is to be used in legal proceedings must be set out so that the person reading it can find what they want for those legal proceedings. A full discussion of the facts and your analysis of them, with a clear conclusion set out, are essential.

Find Out What You Will Be Paid and How Much Time You Will Have to Write the Report

The amount of time you have to write the report and the amount you will be paid are the key parameters. These need to be made clear at the time you receive your instructions. Are you required to provide a Rolls Royce service or a Reliant Robin? If you need more time than you are given, ask for more time. Time limits are vital. If the solicitor misses a court set time limit, the case may be dismissed. This is a prime cause of negligence claims. Be clear when your report is needed.

Fact and Opinion

An expert witness is a witness who gives evidence of facts and his or her opinion on those facts.

There are different sorts of facts: facts observed by the expert – what was said and written, measurements, readings, recordings, results of experiments or inspections. There are also facts reported to the expert by a patient or client or another member of the experts' team. An expert witness gives an opinion about the facts. The expert is entitled to give an opinion because of his/her *qualifications* and/or *experience* in a particular field.

It is essential to have a foundation of facts on which to base an opinion. A reasoned and considered opinion must be based on facts. An opinion which is not supported by factual evidence will be given little weight or credit by the decision maker in court. An example of a fact is that a concrete foundation to a building was one metre thick. An opinion given on this fact by a surveyor is that this was adequate for the building in question. The opinion part in a report is essential for setting out all the possible arguments on a set of facts and illustrating the strengths and weaknesses of those arguments.

Independence of the Expert

An expert witness must give an independent view of the case. An excellent report does not mean one that paints a rosy picture of your client's case. An excellent report is one that clearly sets out the strengths and weaknesses of the case so that the parties know where they stand. As an expert, you are not a hired gun or an advocate. You are a witness.

In *Whitehouse v Jordan* ([1981] 1 WLR 246), Lord Wilberforce stated, "It is necessary that expert evidence presented to the court should be, and should be seen to be, the independent product of the expert, uninfluenced as to form or content by the exigencies of litigation. To the extent that it is not, the evidence is likely to be not only incorrect, but self defeating."

Clearly, it is permissible to seek to persuade the readers of your report that there are more strengths than weaknesses in your opinion, but a report which sets out what the weaknesses are is more credible than one which ignores them. The expert should aim to appear honest and flexible in his/her approach.

THE CONTENT OF AN EXCELLENT REPORT

In Appendix 2 on page 131 is a model report as recommended by Bond Solon Training. This model is only a suggestion and how you create your own personal format will depend on your specialist field. A report is not a letter and should not be set out in the style of a letter, although you should send your report with a covering letter to record that it was sent on a particular date. The following is a suggested format and can be modified to suit your own purposes.

A. Front page

The front page should state that the report is the "Final Report". Do not put that it is the 31st report! Note that you may be asked what you have added or omitted from the earlier reports.

Name
The expert's full name.

Date
The report must be dated the day you sign it and send it to the solicitors. It should not be dated the day you interviewed the patient

or went to the scene; these dates will appear in the report itself. The date indicates that your knowledge is up to date to that date. If anything new comes up, then this can be added.

Field

Set out your specialist field, e.g. plastic surgeon, surveyor, etc.

Party

You must state whether you are giving evidence for the defendant or the plaintiff (in civil cases) or the defendant or the prosecution (in criminal cases).

Solicitors

Give the name of the party you appear to give evidence for, such as Mrs J Bloggs, and the name of the solicitors by whom you are instructed.

Summary of case

Briefly set out the subject matter. For example "this is a breach of contract case involving the supply of heating equipment."

Personal details

You also need to state your own personal details – your name, your professional address, telephone number, fax number and e-mail address if you have one.

References

If the case has already been started by the plaintiff, then ask the solicitors for the court reference number and the title of the action. The names of the parties are also set out, e.g. Smith v Jones in civil cases or R v Brown in criminal cases. The "R" stands for Regina, the Crown.

B. Headers on each page

Set out at the top of each page your name, your specialist field and the name of the party instructing you, including whether it is the plaintiff or defendant.

This means that if any pages are lost or pulled out it is easy to identify them.

C. Contents page

This is essential to give quick access to the report.

D. The main part of the report

1. Introduction

1.01 The writer's full name and specialist field

Do not put in too much detail here. The full details of the expert's qualifications and experience should be set out in an appendix to the report.

It is essential that these full details do go in as they will often be scrutinised by the opposing party's lawyers. It is your experience and qualifications that allow you to give opinion evidence. Do not be modest! Remember, practical experience is just as important as research or publications.

If you are referring to publications, does your opinion in the present case reflect your opinion in the publication? If not, be prepared to explain why your view is different now.

1.02 Summary of case

Give a *short* synopsis of the facts and say what you have been asked to give an opinion on. For example:

The plaintiff was a cyclist knocked off his bicycle by an overtaking car. The plaintiff sustained injuries to his right leg and right arm. I have been asked to provide a medical opinion on the extent of these injuries.

1.03 Summary of conclusions

Do not write a suspense novel. Tell the judge what your conclusion is going to be. This enables the judge to focus on your arguments as he or she reads the report. Your opinion (see paragraph 4 below) is wide ranging, covering all the possibilities and examining strengths and weaknesses in both parties' cases. Your conclusion sets out in brief what you decided, having taken all these factors into account.

1.04 The parties involved

List the people and organisations you will refer to in your report, with a short description of each. This helps the judge to understand the case.

1.05 Technical terms and explanations

Explain that you will put any technical terms in **bold type** and explain them when first used, and also put theses terms in a glossary in the appendix to the report. The glossary should be in alphabetical order.

2. The issues to be addressed

This is not the place to set out your opinion. It is the place to set out clearly what the issues are. If you do not understand what they are, then speak to your instructing solicitors who will help you to determine them. Be clear on whether you are advising on liability (that is who/why the incident was caused), or whether you are advising on quantum (that is the extent of the injury or damage to help the court decide how much money to award the injured party). You may even be providing figures, e.g. accountants may be asked to calculate loss of earnings, loss of pension, etc.

3. The investigation of the facts

This paragraph is for setting out facts alone. Do not mix up the facts with your opinion. This is one of the most common mistakes that expert witnesses make.

It is essential to build up a detailed foundation of facts upon which you will later base your opinion. You should identify separately:

(i) Facts you observed yourself, e.g. from investigations or experiments.

(ii) Facts you were told by a patient or by others working on your behalf.

(iii) Facts which you assumed. Be careful of such assumptions. As far as possible try to establish a fact rather than assume it.

(iv) Opinions of others which you have relied on to form your opinion.

Remember that this is your report and you must be able to justify the foundation of fact upon which you base your opinion.

3.01 Documents

Identify key documents. In the appendix you will have copies of key documents and a list of all the documents you considered in coming to your expert opinion. You may have photocopies of pages from text books.

3.02 Interviews and examinations

Give details of interviews, examinations and inspections. Keep records of the dates and times, and how long they took. Also say who else (if anyone) was present.

3.03 Research

Give details of research you carried out, or research papers you referred to. Copies of these papers should appear in the appendix.

3.04 Experiments

Did you do them? If so, what did you do and what were the results? If someone else did them, say so and say what their qualifications and experience are. Say how you checked the results and how the system in your laboratory works.

4. The opinion

You should set out each of the issues, such as "did the defendant cause the plaintiff injury?", then link these issues with the facts and give your reasoned argument and your opinion on these facts. Do not set out all the facts in detail again in this section.

The opinion is the most important part of your report. You should aim to set out why you think your opinion is right. Highlight the strengths of your argument. If you have seen the other expert's report, set out their opinions or range of opinions briefly. If you have not seen the other party's expert's report, anticipate their opinion. Explain the weaknesses in these opinions.

Address inherent weaknesses in your party's case. The other side will spot them so it is best to acknowledge them and deal with them. It makes your report more credible and independent. Try to look at all the possible arguments that might be put forward and deal with these in your report, e.g. what are all the possible causes of lung cancer? You are being paid to think. Think what the expert called for the other party will say. Try to address these issues in your report and comment on what the other expert will say.

Above all, your intention should be to gain the judge's agreement with the opinion and conclusion of your report.

Do not try to do the judge's job. The judge decides if someone has been negligent, which is a legal term. You are not in a position to say that someone is negligent. You are there to say whether, in your opinion, for example the doctor or the surveyor fell below the standard you as an expert in the field would expect in that situation.

At the end of your opinions, put your conclusion again. The judge needs a conclusion.

E. Signing

Sign and date your report the day you send it to your instructing solicitors. This dates your knowledge at that time. If anything changes, you may need to update your report.

F. Appendices

1. *Experience and qualifications.* Set these out in date order. Explain what your qualifications entail. State any promotions or positions of responsibility you have had. Remember that a judge or jury may not be familiar with the hierarchy in your profession, and explain it.

2. *List of documents examined, copies of key documents.*

3. *List of published material referred to and copies of extracts.*

4. *Photographs, maps, diagrams, models, etc.* These can really help the judge/jury understand technical areas of the case. It is not usually possible to turn up with these things at the trial. Copies must be provided to the other party on disclosure. All such documents must be clearly labelled. It is useful to have cross-references in the report to the documents or visual aids.

5. *Chronology of events.*

6. *Glossary of technical terms* (set this out in alphabetical order).

7. *Lord Woolf declaration.**

8. *Others.*

* See Bond Solon's model report in the appendix for details of this. It states that you understand that your duty as an expert witness is to assist the court, giving honest independent opinion. It also says that you have undertaken a truthful disclosure of all relevant facts that affect the validity of the report.

THE FORM OF AN EXCELLENT REPORT

The form, or way a report looks, is very important. It is an essential tool to aid settlement of the case or the decision at a trial. It must be accessible, that is easy for people to find their way around. It should enable them to understand what the case is about. It should clearly set out your opinion. Poorly presented and organised documents can slow down the progress of the trial. It will be irritating for the judge if he or she cannot find their way around the report and it will be embarrassing for you if you cannot find your way around your report and direct the court to important areas of it.

The presentation of the report can affect the weight given to its contents.

Aim to present complex ideas in a way that can be understood. State the obvious and use simple, clear language. Your report is an essential tool for the judge to use in reaching his/her decision.

The following are tips on how to present your report:

1. Use **clear headings** – clearly define where you have set out a summary of the facts, your opinion and your conclusion.

2. Have a **contents page**, with reference to page numbers and/or paragraph numbers.

3. Use **page numbers** and **paragraph numbers**. Make sure cross-references to the appendices are included and are accurate.

4. Have **headers** on each page.

5. Have a **front page** which is visible through a transparent cover. This sets out vital details about the case.

6. Make sure there is a **clear conclusion**, which is your conclusion. Do not let the lawyers push you into writing a

conclusion you do not agree with. You will come unstuck under vigorous cross-examination if you did not come to that conclusion on the facts. You must be independent.

7. Include a **chronology** to help the judge. A useful chronology is a list of all the dates that you examined a patient, or visited a site.

8. Include a **synopsis – a summary of the facts**. This will help the judge to focus on the relevant facts and understand what the case is about.

9. Make sure your report is **signed** by you personally and is **dated** the day you send it to the solicitors.

10. Include a **glossary** of technical terms that are used in the appendices.

11. Include **graphics**, photographs, diagrams or models that will help the judge understand the case.

12. Separate **fact** from **opinion**.

13. Do not allow the lawyers to rewrite your report for you. They can change the emphasis of your opinion. Also it is easy for the judge to spot the style used by lawyers.

14. Write in the first person – "I"; it is your report, you sign it. Even if a team of people within a company have worked on a report, one person will have to be the expert witness (or if there are several areas of expertise, one person from each area of expertise). A report should not be signed in the company's name.

At a planning enquiry, the director of a company may have to write a final report in which he has to give his opinion on why an electricity pylon should be put in a particular place. He will include in his report the facts and opinions given to him by a range of other experts, such as an environmental expert, a construction engineer, a geologist and a civil engineer. Although the report includes facts and opinions from a number of people, it is not a joint report, signed by several people. However, each of these individuals may be asked to write separate reports and each may be called to give evidence in their own field of expertise.

15. Set out your **qualifications** and **experience** in full in the appendices. Make what you set out relevant to the case that you are giving your expert opinion in. Your qualifications should be briefly explained – do not just set out a string of letters. Your experience should outline the number of years' experience you have in a particular field and the level of that experience. If you refer to positions of responsibility, explain them clearly. Mention any publications or research you have undertaken. Concentrate on your most recent and relevant experience.

16. Use A4 good quality **paper** which is hole punched and place two-inch **margins** around the paper to leave room for the judge to make notes. Use double spacing between the lines. It makes it easier to read.

17. **Binding**. There is no need to use leather! A slide binder keeps the pages together between two plastic covers, one for the front and one for the back. Avoid comb binders as these make it difficult to photocopy the report.

18. **Printing**. Use a laser printer if possible.

19. Check the **accuracy** of the report. Mistakes, typing errors or wrong dates look bad. In cross-examination, the lawyers may seek to embarrass you by picking up on mistakes.

20. Make sure your final report is a **stand-alone report**. The judge should have everything he or she needs to make a decision in one report.

If you have written a number of reports or supplementary reports, then you should rationalise them into your final report. Only very minor, last minute points are acceptable in a supplementary report form.

For example, if you write a report on injuries to a patient after your first examination and then you examine the patient 6 or 12 months later, your findings in these first and second examinations should be together in your final report. The judge does not want to have to read two separate opinions.

21. Finally, find out from your solicitor **how many copies** of your report are needed and print off that many and send them. This avoids poor quality, scruffy photocopies of your report being used.

THE WRITING PROCESS

Treat your report as a sales opportunity, to "sell" you as an expert witness and to "sell" your opinion. Other lawyers may be impressed by your report and instruct you in other cases. Most importantly, you want the judge to be impressed by your report because once (s)he has read it (s)he understands the issues, the facts and why you have reached the opinion that you have. You want to write in order to persuade the judge to agree with your opinion.

Remember that it is not what you write that matters, it is what the reader understands. Try to present the report in a way that is easy to understand. It is your responsibility to communicate and to take care of the reader of the report. Remember that the judge/jury and lawyers are not experts in your field. Write in a simple, clear way which will enable them to understand what the issues are and why you have reached your opinion. It may help to explain other possible opinions but then illustrate why these are not as creditable as your opinion. Aim to give a good overall picture.

Make sure you remain independent – see a distinction between yourself as an expert witness giving evidence and the lawyers who represent the parties. Also see a difference between yourself as a person and as the writer of the report. Stand back from your report and hear in your mind all the arguments that could be put forward against your opinion. Try to counter these arguments in the report.

Writer's block can be helped by writing what comes to you first and not bothering about the order. You should write all your report and then rewrite it. Do not try to write and edit at the same time. The final version will probably be shorter than the first version. As you edit it ask if each sentence gives any further meaning; go through asking "What does this say? Does it add anything?"

Chapter 4

THE EXPERT IN COURT

SUMMARY

● The expert's role ●

● Technical preparation ●

● Personal preparation ●

● What happens in court ●

● What happens in the witness box ●

● Giving evidence and handling cross-examination ●

● Recognising and dealing with lawyers' techniques ●

● How to direct your answers ●

● The qualities of good evidence giving ●

● Finding out the result ●

In this chapter, the word "court" is used to include any formal legal forum, e.g. tribunals, arbitrations, investigations and planning enquiries, and the word "judge" to refer to the decision maker.

THE EXPERT'S ROLE IN COURT

The expert witness is not in court to win the case, that is the job of the lawyers who are advocates but do not give evidence. Although the expert is instructed and paid by one side, his/her role is to give independent evidence and not be a hired gun. You should be objective and impartial. You are there to give honest, independent professional opinion. You must maintain your integrity and tell the truth, the whole truth and nothing but the truth.

83

Your good name is your greatest asset as an expert witness. Do not distort your opinion to "win" one case.

You can, however, work to the best of your ability for your instructing solicitors. You can bring out the strengths in the factual evidence from which you reached your opinion, and point out the weaknesses in the arguments put forward by the other party's expert.

Your primary function is to assist the court in reaching its decision. You need to be able to explain the technical aspects of your opinion in a clear, confident, succinct and interesting way. You are trying to persuade the judge or jury that your opinion is the best one on a given set of facts.

WHAT THE JUDGE WANTS

To fully understand your role it is useful to understand how the judge approaches the evidence of an expert witness.

This is best summarised by Stuart Smith L.J. who described in *Loveday v Renton* ([1990] 1 Med LR 177 at 125) how the judge will approach the evidence of an expert witness:

"This involves an examination of the reasons given for his opinions and the extent to which they are supported by the evidence. The judge also has to decide what weight to attach to a witness's opinion by examining the internal consistency and logic of his evidence. The care with which he has considered the subject and presented his evidence; his precision and accuracy of thought as demonstrated by his answers; how he responds to searching and informed cross-examination, and in particular the extent to which a witness faces up to and accepts the logic of a proposition put in cross-examination or is prepared to concede points that are seen to be correct; the extent to which a witness has conceived an opinion and is reluctant to re-examine it in the light of later evidence, or demonstrates a flexibility of mind which may involve changing or modifying opinions previously held; whether or not a witness is biased or lacks independence ..."

Clearly, a well prepared report (see Chapter 3) goes a long way towards showing a logical approach, highlighting facts and opinions, and strengths and weaknesses in the various experts' opinions. However, it is important that you maintain this clear, logical, calm approach while giving evidence.

The judge has a difficult job in deciding cases (as does a jury in a criminal trial). The judge needs to trust you as someone who is believable and who can materially assist him or her in deciding the case. Judges are worried about making the wrong decision and whether their decision may be appealed. They want the expert to help them come to the right decision.

The judge may not know about your field and, in any event, will not know as much as you, the expert witness. If the judge or the barristers did have your knowledge, you would not be needed. You are there in the role of an educator, someone to help the non-experts understand a difficult area. It may help to think of good teachers you knew and model yourself on the way they taught difficult concepts.

You are *very important; you are a key witness*. You examined the patient or the DNA samples – the court wants to hear your evidence. The judge needs to hear you clearly and understand your evidence. The biggest compliment you can be paid by the judge is "Thank you, I understand the case now!"

What the Judge is Thinking

Once you arrive at court do not *concern* yourself with what the judge is thinking about you. Regard the judge as being neutral. You cannot alter the judge's preconceptions about whether female experts are better than male experts, or whether experts who wear glasses are better than those who do not. Once in court, concentrate on yourself and your evidence giving. You should only think about dress and appearance *before* you go to court (see below).

PREPARATION FOR THE HEARING

When Does Preparation Start?

Preparation for a trial does not start a few days or even a few weeks before the trial. Preparation for trial starts as soon as you, the expert, receive instructions from the solicitors, and every telephone call, letter or note should be thought of in that context.

Even though you may be asked at this stage to prepare a preliminary report or a final report, be aware that the case might end up in court.

Also be aware that every day in your job as a doctor, nurse, surveyor or DNA analyst, your findings and notes could be the subject of later court proceedings. Make sure you keep proper notes of what you have done, when and why. Record reasons for professional decisions.

Technical Preparation

1. **It is essential that you carry out a detailed, vigorous investigation/research into the facts of the case.** You need to get as much *evidence* of *fact* as you can. When doing your investigation, have an open mind. Gather all the facts. You must build a foundation of fact upon which to base your opinion. An opinion which is not based on fact will be an opinion that can quickly be shot down in court.

Your facts may come in many different forms. Some facts you will have observed or measured yourself, some you will have been told by a patient (for example), some you will have been told by people in your research team who carried out the investigation. You must say *where* the facts came from. Distinguish between facts you observed and facts you were told.

2. **Make sure you get *all the available information* from your solicitors.** Some lawyers may try to shape the result of your findings by only giving you some of the information. This can be disastrous if at trial an opposing barrister puts to you in cross-examination evidence you have not seen before.

   Keep asking the lawyers if they have any more documents or witness statements, especially after disclosure. *Be proactive.*

   Do not rely on the lawyers to spot the issues. They may have little grasp of the issues within a specialist field. You are the expert, you are being *paid* to give an expert opinion.

   Ensure that you are up to date on all your information and/or update your report.

3. **Create a working relationship with the lawyers.** Do not be afraid to ask them if you do not understand what you are supposed to be doing. Help the lawyers to understand the technicalities of the case. This will help both your and their preparation. Train the lawyers, particularly the barristers, to ask you the right questions. Note that this is not the same as the lawyers training you to give particular answers! Help the lawyers to formulate questions to ask the expert(s) called by the other party. You will be able to spot the weaknesses in their evidence. Remember, often barristers will only have the papers for a short time before trial. You should insist on meeting your party's barrister before the trial. Ask your instructing solicitors to

arrange a "conference with counsel". This is a meeting at which you can discuss the main issues in the case.

4. **Write your report** (see Chapter 3). Make sure it is independent. Do not change your opinion under pressure from the lawyers. If your opinion changes from the time you wrote the report to the time the case is to be heard in court, tell the lawyers. Be very clear in your recommendations and conclusions in your report. It will help to focus your oral evidence giving.

5. **Identify the strengths and weaknesses in the case.** Look at all the possible arguments. DO NOT LEAVE ALL THE THINKING UNTIL YOU GET TO COURT. Think of likely questions that will be put in cross-examination. Remember that the cross-examining barrister will ask critical questions designed to expose the weaknesses in your opinion. Be ready to turn away from weaknesses and play to strengths in your case.

Remember – cases are really won out of court, not in court. This preparation is vital.

6. **Prepare any graphs, plans, photographs or visual displays that will help the judge/jury understand your evidence.** Do not leave doing this until the last moment. If you do, the other party may not allow you to use it. Let the lawyers know what visual aids you will need to use in court well in advance. As you write your report, think how you will explain what you are writing about; this will help you think of visual displays that may be useful.

7. **Make sure your files and documents are in good order and correctly paginated.** This will enable you to remain in control of your evidence giving. Remember to use your report to illustrate why you have reached your opinion.

8. **Ensure you are familiar with documents. Re-read notes and, most importantly, re-read your report.** Evidence giving is not a memory test but you need to be able to find your way around your report, quickly and accurately. This will avoid you becoming flustered. It helps to be able to point out to the judge diagrams, research notes, etc. in your report. This reinforces your opinion. Do not annotate your report even though you may want to highlight parts. It looks strange if you annotate it and the judge or lawyers may ask you to refer to the court copy of the report not the one you take into the box.

9. **Keep an indexed record of all your published work.** You may be asked questions about this in court. Be prepared to talk about your qualifications and experience, they give you credit as an expert – they outline the area of your expertise. Think of phrases that describe your qualifications and experience concisely and powerfully.

10. **Prepare a chronology, if necessary.** A list of times and dates can be useful if there are many details to go through.

Personal Preparation

1. **Agree your fees as soon as possible,** including fees for cancelled appearances.

2. **Make a list of all the things you need to take with you to court.** For example, your report, documents, visual aids.

3. **Visit a court** and sit in on a court hearing – preferably the court where you will be giving evidence – so you can see the layout and procedure. Ask your lawyers to give you as many tips as they can about who will be in court, what a particular barrister is like, etc.

4. **Find out when the trial is and how long it is going to last** and how long you might be expected to give evidence for. Lawyers will know, especially in civil cases, some time before the trial what dates the trial is likely to be. This is because they will be given a fixed date for it or will at least know when it has appeared in the "warned list", that is that it could be called in for trial any day soon.

5. **Find out *where* the court is and *how* you will get there**, e.g. by train, bus or car. Is there parking available, etc? Find out *when* you need to be there and where to go when you get there. Some courts (e.g. the High Court in the Strand) are like rabbit warrens. It is best to *arrange to meet* your instructing solicitors at a particular place and time so they can take you to the relevant courtroom. Ask where you can get food or drinks and where the lavatories are.

6. **Clear your diary** and sort out your domestic arrangements. Make sure you allow for far more time in court than is initially suggested. Trials tend to last longer than originally planned, particularly if there are adjournments.

7. **Plan what you are going to wear!** Make sure that you have some changes of clothes if you are going to be giving evidence for several days. Wear smart, sober professional clothes – dark suits, white or pale plain shirts or blouses. Women should avoid jazzy dangling earrings (as should men!). Ties should be sober. Jackets look best buttoned up. The most important thing is to feel comfortable and professional. Imagine you are dressing for an important job interview. Remember that lawyers dress in a sober fashion and that you do not want to look out of place in the courtroom.

8. **Decide how you want to come across and get colleagues to give you some feedback.** You should want to come across as

professional and competent, honest, helpful, cool, calm and collected, unbiased, clear and informative, interesting, reliable, credible, caring and a true expert. You do not want to come across as defensive, pompous, arrogant or nervous.

A good idea is to prepare your introduction to the court – that is your name, professional address, qualifications and experience – and rehearse this and get a colleague to comment on how you are coming across.

9. Try some **techniques for relaxation and confidence**. For example, visualise yourself in court giving evidence with confidence and power.

10. **Be aware of the date of the trial**. Tell the lawyers well in advance dates that are difficult for you because you are on holiday or giving evidence in another trial. Keep the lawyers updated on a three-monthly basis on difficult dates. It may be possible to arrange the trial around these dates. As soon as you receive the letter telling you the date of the trial, book the time in your diary. If for some reason it is impossible for you to go on that date, tell the solicitor immediately. Notify your employer and any other people who have been helping you in the case preparation, of the trial date.

11. **Attend a training course on giving evidence.** This will help your confidence enormously, whether you have given evidence before or not.

Preparation on the Day Before Going to Court

Review your notes again and ensure that all your information is clear in your mind. Prepare everything you need for your appearance to avoid rushing around on the day itself. Phone your solicitor to confirm the meeting time and check your diary is clear and that all your colleagues are covering your work, etc. Finally, have a relaxing evening and an early night!

On the Day You Go to Court

Arrive at court early and meet your lawyers. Find out where the waiting room is and any other facilities, such as the lavatories and refreshment area. Tell your solicitor where you will be.

As an expert witness, you will usually be allowed to sit in court to watch. A witness of fact has to wait outside the court. Your place is usually behind your lawyers. You can help prompt the lawyers by making notes of questions to ask the other party's expert witness. Write any questions on a clean sheet of paper, date and time it and pass it forward. The barrister can look at it when ready so you do not interrupt the flow of his or her advocacy.

Check with your solicitor who you can and cannot speak to. Generally, you should not talk to the other witnesses or parties in the case.

WHAT HAPPENS IN COURT

Layout of the Courtroom

The judge will be at one end of the room, sitting behind a bench on a raised platform. (In criminal trials in the Crown Court, there will be a jury as well as the judge; the jury sits in a separate area. In Magistrates Courts' there will be three lay magistrates, i.e. non lawyers, or a stipendiary magistrate sitting alone, and a legally qualified clerk. In tribunals there will be a panel of usually three people. Usually one is legally qualified.)

Directly in front of the judge will sit the clerks and officials. The witness box will be at the side of the room, and is usually raised and square. The lawyers sit behind tables facing the bench (i.e. the judge). At the front will be the barristers, behind them the solicitors and expert witnesses. Members of the public may be sitting in the public gallery and there may be press present in court.

Before your first court appearance, you should visit a courtroom to see how things work and the way everything is positioned.

The Order of the Proceedings

(See Chapter 1 for detail on procedure and personnel in criminal and civil trials.)

1. The barristers will make an opening speech explaining their version of events.

2. The plaintiff presents his/her case (through the lawyers). The plaintiff's witnesses will be called to the witness box and each will be questioned by the plaintiff's lawyers and then cross-examined by the defence.

3. The defence then present their case, calling their witnesses for examination and cross-examination.

4. The lawyers each summarise the evidence they have presented (closing speech).

5. The judge gives his or her decision.

WHAT HAPPENS IN THE WITNESS BOX?

As a general rule, witnesses of fact cannot take notes or statements into the witness box. Expert witnesses are allowed to look at their reports and other documents but if you need to refer to notes during your evidence giving, your lawyer will have to ask permission from the judge. All the documents to be used at the trial by any witnesses will be contained in the court bundle. If you need to see any of these documents, you will be given the bundle.

When it is time to give your evidence, you will be called by one of the court officers. You may already be sitting in court. You should stand up in the witness box, although you may sit down with the permission of the judge, after you have taken the oath/affirmation.

You will be asked to take the *oath* or *affirmation.*

The Oath and Affirmation

The oath is a promise on the Bible or other holy book to tell the truth. The affirmation is simply a promise to tell the truth, not based on a holy book. Decide before you go to court whether you wish to swear or affirm. It is *entirely* up to you which you choose to do – they carry equal weight. You will be asked to read the words from a card or paper in front of you and, if swearing the oath, to hold the holy book in your uplifted right hand. Take your time to read slowly, clearly and audibly, facing the judge. Stand still with your feet slightly apart and your legs straight. Do not look up while reading from the card.

The Oath – "I swear by Almighty God that the evidence I shall give shall be the truth, the whole truth and nothing but the truth" (for the Bible; different wording is used for other holy books).

The Affirmation – "I do solemnly, sincerely and truly declare and affirm that the evidence I shall give shall be the truth, the whole truth and nothing but the truth."

Examination in Chief

The purpose of the examination in chief is to enable the judge to hear the witness's oral evidence in his/her own words. The examination in chief will start with you giving your name and professional address; sometimes the barrister will ask you to state your name and address, sometimes they will just ask you to confirm it. You will be asked "Is this your report?" The judge will already have read the report.

You will also be asked to talk about your qualifications and experience. They must be accurate. Do not be modest – this is your opportunity to outline your expertise. Remember that you are being paid for your expertise so this is no time to hide it. Concentrate on the area of your expertise that is relevant to the case; it is useful to outline your experience in chronological order. For example, say how long you have been an accountant, say how long you have been a partner, and say what experience you have in the particular area that the court trial is about. You may wish to refer the judge to your detailed curriculum vitae which is in the appendix to your report.

When giving your evidence, make sure you stay within the field of your expertise. It is all too easy to comment on matters just outside the circle of your expertise but it is dangerous and not the reason you are in court.

In criminal trials, you will be asked a lot of questions to bring out the evidence in your report. In civil cases, the judge may have read your report and will simply ask you to confirm that it is accurate, up to date and that you still agree with it.

Cross-Examination

The purpose of the cross-examination is for the other side to test your evidence. The other party's barrister will try to show that your information and opinion are inaccurate or will try to elicit evidence that is beneficial to their case. Cross-examination is a hostile process, in keeping with an adversarial system, and you should expect critical questions and, in particular, attacks on your credibility as an expert and on your expert opinion. Remember that it is the duty of the cross-examining barrister to test your evidence and this can feel quite painful – or you may enjoy it as an intellectual challenge.

Re-Examination

This does not always take place. If it does, it is an opportunity for your lawyers to clarify something that may have been discussed during cross-examination. *You may be recalled after your evidence has been given.*

You will then be told that you can leave the witness box and, if you are a witness of fact, whether you are released from court and free to go home.

The ideal expert is one who can sit in court before and after their evidence has been given, especially when the other experts give evidence. This means that you can advise the barristers on the weakness of the other party's expert evidence. However, you will only be asked to do this if the client or Legal Aid Board can afford to pay you for your time.

YOUR EVIDENCE AND CROSS-EXAMINATION

As an expert witness, you are in court to give evidence of your expert opinion. This is the important thing. Try to see yourself as separate from your evidence.

The job of the lawyers, usually barristers, representing the other party is to test and discredit your evidence. The lawyers do this in cross-examination, the name given to questions put by the opposing party's lawyers.

The lawyer who cross-examines you will often seem to be attacking you personally. Do not take any of the points raised in cross-examination personally; the lawyer is just doing his or her job. There is no need for the expert to get cross, angry or defensive. You should never get into an argument with the barrister.

As soon as you allow the barrister to get "under your skin", you may lose control of calm, professional evidence giving. The quality of the evidence you give will be affected if you are flustered and angry and trying to score points.

Attacking you personally is just one of the techniques that a lawyer will use to undermine your evidence. In particular, the opposing lawyer will try to undermine your credibility as an expert witness by attacking your qualifications and experience or by attacking your opinion. The lawyer will have had the weaknesses in your opinion pointed out to them by their expert. They will put these weaknesses to you. They will try to show that you have not got a reasoned basis for your opinion. Ensure that you outline the facts that support your opinion. An expert who states an opinion just because his lawyers suggested it will be found out!

There are various methods of testing a witness in cross-examination, but the following are common techniques:

1. Trying to limit the expert's expertise by showing that the expert's qualifications and experience are inferior (for example "Why did you only attend X institution to study for your degree and not Oxbridge") or do not apply to the case in question.

   The expert must be prepared to explain how and why his/her qualifications and expertise are relevant.

2. Unfavourable comparisons with another expert. This will be done by suggesting the other expert is better qualified or more experienced, for example "Our expert has 25 years' experience in the field, you only have 10. How can you say our expert is

wrong?". Don't be daunted by this, take time to explain your own experience and qualifications and the strengths of your opinion.

3. Asking the expert to explain jargon or technical terms. The expert should be prepared to explain simply and clearly any technical terms (s)he uses without waiting to be asked to explain them. If you use them, explain them straight away.

4. Criticism of the expert's investigation and research process. Methods may be attacked and any omissions or errors pointed out.

5. Suggesting that their expert's opinion is within a reasonable band of opinions and you cannot disagree that that opinion is legitimate. Agree it may be legitimate, but illustrate why your opinion may be better!

6. Trying to get you to agree with some of what the other expert says.

7. Attacking your opinion for not being based on a sound foundation of fact. Always illustrate which facts you took into account when reaching your opinion.

8. Hypothetical situations may be suggested to illustrate weaknesses in your opinion. Make sure you distinguish between the actual facts and the hypothetical facts when giving your answer.

9. Trying to get the expert to become extreme or unreasonable in their view to show bias. Do not exaggerate; do not say you are absolutely 100% certain, for few things are this certain. Remain flexible but firm. Never say "never" or "always".

The lawyer is trained to control you, the expert witness, in cross-examination. You must remain calm and confident. *Do not* become defensive or argumentative. Play to your strengths. Avoid letting the lawyer take control.

Remember your role in court is to help, and in some cases to educate, the judge. The judge is also neutral – talk to the judge, not to the barrister asking the questions. This will help you to remain calm and to avoid getting cross with or upset by the barrister's questions. The judge may ask questions to help understand the case.

Do not be afraid of lawyers. Realise you are both professionals in court to do a job and that your roles are different.

Who To Talk To

You should always talk to the decision maker, who is the judge or jury in a Crown Court and the magistrate(s) in a Magistrates' Court. It is the decision maker who needs to hear your evidence. Whenever you answer a lawyer's question, turn to the judge before speaking. Use the turning technique described below to help you do this.

If your evidence in the witness box is interrupted by a lunch or over-night adjournment, do not speak to anyone about the case without authority from the court. This includes your instructing solicitor.

What To Say

Tell the truth. If you cannot remember, say so. If you do not know the answer, say so. Explain your answers if you want to. For example, why you decided, as an accountant assessing income loss, to use a particular multiplier; why as an actuary you chose 1% not 2%.

Do not comment on things about which you have no direct knowledge, for example what you think the doctor thought. Stay within your field of knowledge and expertise. If the question goes outside this area, say so and explain why you cannot answer.

LAWYERS' TECHNIQUES AND TYPICAL QUESTIONS

It is impossible to predict exactly what a lawyer will ask you in court. Nor is your own lawyer allowed to "coach" you through your evidence by practising with you beforehand.

There are two areas that need to be considered: examination in chief and cross-examination.

In Examination in Chief

Your lawyer asks these questions. The questions are likely to follow the order of your statement or report, and you should feel free to set the pace of your answers, giving as much relevant information as you can. This is your opportunity to put across the strengths of your expert opinion. During the examination in chief, your lawyer cannot ask you "leading questions", i.e. a question that suggests the answer. The lawyer must get you to volunteer the information in your statement or report.

In civil cases the examination in chief can be very short as the judge will have read your report and this reading can replace the examination in chief; you may just be asked if there are any additions.

In Cross-Examination

Cross-examination is by the other side's lawyer. As mentioned, they are seeking to discredit your evidence and so will be keen to confuse you and try to get you to contradict yourself. They will ask questions about your weaknesses not your strengths. The lawyer's tactics will be to attack the content of your evidence or occasionally to undermine you by theatrics. The overall techniques used were described in the previous section.

Below are some further examples of lawyers' tricks and techniques.

- Asking closed questions – *"Did you see the patient walk or not? Answer the question yes or no"*.

- Feigning ignorance or confusion – *"How could you listen to the doctor if you were talking to the patient?"*

- Using patronising tones and sarcasm – *"Well, of course you would say that, because he is paying your fees today"*.

- Making direct attacks on the ability of an expert witness – *"What made you think you could act; you've only had 18 months' experience, why didn't you get help? ... What made you think you were properly qualified to do this job?"*

- Using multiple questions – *"What time did the patient arrive, what did she say, what did the nurse do when she saw the patient"*.

- Interrupting you mid-sentence – especially if you are just about to make a good point.

- Giving looks of disbelief or using a tone of disbelief.

- Shuffling papers, passing notes or whispering to colleagues.

- Focusing on tiny, irrelevant points such as an unimportant time.

- Repeating earlier questions, in the hope you will contradict yourself.

- Mispronouncing your name – *"Well Ms Frompton/Trumpton/ Frumptin"*.

- Contradicting you, especially by using your opponent's expert's opinion.

- Remaining silent. You will perhaps want to fill the gap.

- Using hypothetical questions – *"What if the concrete had been two inches thicker?"*

- Jumping around in the chronology, starting at the end of your report and working backwards.

- Using jargon and asking you to explain it.

- Picking on inaccuracies in your report, e.g. typos, dates.

- Picking on inconsistencies between what you say and what other experts say.

- Asking you to speak up or slow down.

- Getting you to agree to absolutes – *"Are you 100% certain?"*

Before the case, take time to think of likely questions or lines of "attack". Write a list in your court file. The key is how to handle these questions so that you say what you want to say. This is discussed below.

KEEPING IN CONTROL AND HANDLING LAWYERS' TECHNIQUES

You are the one in control. There are two very good reasons for this. The first is that, no matter how well prepared the lawyers are, they do not know your field or evidence as well as you do. They are not experts in your field. They were not there and thus did not see it, do it or hear it, investigate or research it. You were and did! All the information the lawyer has is, at best, "second hand".

The second reason why you are in charge of your evidence is that the judge wants to hear your information. The better the information you give the judge, the easier it is for him or her to make a decision.

With that control in mind, how do you deal with the techniques? Identify the strengths and weaknesses in your evidence. Think in advance what the key points of your evidence are and take *every opportunity* to get them over to the court so that the court receives a balanced view of the case.

Listen to the question – often it is designed to focus on a weakness. Think how you can present your best points in answer to the question. See every question as being a **gift** which enables you to put forward the strongest points in your evidence.

Do not be distracted by the techniques. Treat them as opportunities. If the lawyer is repeating a question, say so – "Yes, that was the point I dealt with earlier". Or if it is a long, meandering question, help the judge by breaking it down – "Well, there are three points here" or "It actually happened in this order". Ignore sarcasm and bullying. If you are asked to answer a question "Yes" or "No" you do not have to. The lawyer is asking you to do this to push you into extreme views. Say to the judge "I can't answer the question yes or no, there are a number of factors that have to be considered ...".

Do not agree to absolutes, e.g. "never" or "100%". Be careful in giving estimates in relation to time, space or distance.

Take your time. Remember you are the one in control. The judge is there to see fair play. Ask the judge if you need more time to answer the question, or if you need the question repeated. In other words, do not be afraid to take charge of your information and present it in the way that you want.

Remember that the lawyers are only doing their job in using their techniques. When you visit a court and see some cross-examination in action, separate the technique from the question. For example, see that there were three looks of disbelief, two multiple questions, a long pause and so forth.

HOW TO DIRECT YOUR ANSWERS

Remember the only person to speak to in court is the judge or magistrates (and jury in criminal cases in the Crown Court). They make the decision. Do not try to persuade the questioning lawyer, or even speak to him/her. A good way of remembering this is as follows:

- As soon as you get into the witness box, directly face the judge and point your feet at him/her. If there is a jury, include both judge and jury.

- Do not move your feet. Now twist at your hips to face the lawyer.

- Look at the lawyer and listen carefully to the question. Look for a gift for you in the question and watch out for any techniques that may be used to disconcert you.

- When the lawyer has finished his or her question, and not before, turn back to face the judge/jury. The fact that your feet are pointing that way will remind you. You have a few moments in the turning to prepare your answer. In any event, you should never hurry your answer.

- When you are directly facing the judge/jury, give your answer. You can see if the judge is with you or if you are speaking too quickly as (s)he may be writing down your answer. Do not worry if (s)he is not looking at you if (s)he is writing.

- When you have finished your answer, turn back to the lawyer slowly. This signals you are ready for the next question. If the lawyer tries to interrupt you, continue facing the judge/jury and continue with your answer.

Although this may sound unnatural, it is very easy with practice and will give you a lot of control in the speed of the questions. The judge/

jury can also hear better and you will not be tempted to get into a conversation with the lawyer.

Be sure to use this technique in the witness box. It is straightforward and extremely effective in allowing you to focus on the judge/jury and ignore the lawyer when giving your answer.

HOW TO KEEP CALM

There are various techniques you can use and may already know about. The most obvious and perhaps most important is to look after yourself, especially in the days preceding the trial.

Another tip is to use visualisation. This is a technique many successful people use, particularly sportsmen and women and business people. It involves sitting somewhere quiet where you will not be disturbed. Close your eyes, take some deep breaths and, in your mind, imagine being the way you want to be, fulfilling the criteria you have written on your list of how you want to come across. Imagine yourself remaining this way through the cross-examination, whether it is slow, quick, aggressive, calm or straightforward. You can practise this as many times as you like. When you get into the witness box for real, you will have already rehearsed your evidence and you will feel more confident because it is not completely unfamiliar to your brain. If you have not tried this kind of technique before, do try it. It is very powerful.

Use the support you have around you – friends, family or colleagues. It is a cliché, but sharing a problem or fear can often get things into perspective. Attend a confidence-building training course in courtroom skills. Remember also that even the most experienced witnesses can be nervous before going to court. Some barristers are even physically ill! You are only human.

THE QUALITIES OF GOOD EVIDENCE GIVING

Your evidence consists of two parts: the content, which is largely set out in your report, and the presentation. Use your report to help you and the judge when you are in court.

The essence of good evidence giving is simple, clear communication. Be helpful, truthful and independent. Be a reliable source of information. The way in which you give your evidence affects the weight of credibility attached to it. Imagine that, if your evidence is clear, succinct, convincing and truthful, it will weigh down heavily on the scales of justice to help tip the balance in the favour of the party who has instructed you. If, however, your evidence is confusing and you are nervous, aggressive, pompous, rambling and inflexible then it will be given little or no weight.

Research suggests that juries, in particular, are influenced by the *way* evidence is given rather than the evidence itself. You need to get both the evidence and the presentation right to be as effective as possible.

About You

Aim to be friendly, warm and helpful. Do not see being an expert witness as an opportunity to be pompous and egotistical.

Listen carefully to a question and look at the questioner. Do not answer until the barrister has finished the question and you are sure you understand it. Stand up straight with your weight balanced evenly on both feet. Do not hop from foot to foot or jig around as this distracts from your evidence giving. It also makes you appear nervous. Decide where you are going to put your hands. Do not put them in your pockets. It is often best to rest them lightly on the top of the witness box. Do not grip the edge of the witness box.

Try to appear relaxed. Maintain friendly open eye contact with the judge/jury. Though you may be able to sit down, it is customary to stand until invited to sit.

Make sure you do justice to yourself. Explain your qualifications and experience with pride. Highlight those areas of your qualifications and experience that really help with the case before the court.

Your Voice: Speed of Evidence

The voice is an important tool in evidence giving. Smiling before you go into court helps to relax the muscles in the face. This gives you more control over your voice. Holding your breath is a natural reaction to stress but it will make your voice quiver. Breathe. It will calm you down and slow you down. You must control the *speed* of your evidence giving. A good tip is to watch the judge's pen (or other presiding officer's) as they may take notes as you speak.

Make your voice interesting by altering the pitch and volume. You can use your voice to emphasise important points. Speak rather than nodding or shrugging. Avoid reading documents at the same time as speaking. If necessary, ask for a few minutes to be allowed to read the document or report.

How to Present Evidence

Use simple, short sentences. Repetition will help ensure your key points are heard. Do not use technical language or convoluted sentences. Imagine yourself as a teacher; state the obvious and explain technical areas.

Make sure you are consistent and logical in your thought process. Consider carefully matters put to you in questions. Concede some points; for example, if asked "Would it have been better to look at 100 samples rather than 10", agree it would. But say you are confident that, with 10, you have the right answer. Be ready to be flexible but do not be bullied into changing your opinion.

If you say something that is incorrect, take the earliest opportunity to correct it.

Refer to your report as much as you can. This will encourage the judge to annotate his/her copy and refer to it when preparing his/her judgment.

The Content of the Evidence

An expert witness gives evidence of both fact and opinion. As seen in Chapter 1, facts come from many sources. It is critical that you should distinguish between facts and opinion when giving oral evidence, in the same way as you distinguish between facts and opinion in your report.

You need to refer back to your foundation of fact before you give your opinion evidence. Thus a surveyor might refer back to the depth of concrete that he measured before saying that, in his opinion, this was insufficient for a particular building.

Do not make assumptions from one set of facts that cannot be supported by another. For example, do not assume the base cracked because the building was too heavy.

It is very important that, in giving your opinion evidence, you **stay within your field of expertise**. It is very easy to be pulled outside the circle of your expertise and to attempt to answer questions. Sooner or later you will be caught out.

Examples are: the general practitioner who attempts to answer questions on psychology or open heart surgery; the accountant who tries to answer questions on the world economy; the nurse who tries to give evidence on the biological/chemical make-up of the brain.

Finally, you must make sure that you bring out the *strengths* of your case under cross-examination. Expert witnesses frequently complain that during cross-examination they were asked all the wrong questions! It is up to you to make sure you bring out the strong points.

You must take control. Do not let the barristers control you. You must take responsibility for getting a fair picture across to the judge/jury. Be as persuasive as you can. Remember that different experts have different opinions. Do not be put off by the fact that another expert has a different opinion.

HOW TO DEAL WITH THE OTHER EXPERTS' EVIDENCE

There will usually be an expert witness called by each of the parties.

An expert witness must be prepared to *comment* on another expert witness's opinion. This can be done in the expert report, which can be updated if necessary, or in oral evidence given in court at the trial. The expert should anticipate in his/her report what the opinion of another expert might be. The weaknesses of their opinion can then be highlighted. It is important to remember that the fact that the expert witness has a different opinion does not mean that one opinion is wrong and the other right. It is often a question of which opinion is more likely to reflect the position accurately. Be prepared to substantiate the strength of the facts that support your expert opinion. Also try to highlight the weaknesses in the facts relied on by the other expert in reaching their opinion.

Do not completely discount the evidence of another expert. Remember, it is important to be professional at all times and that opinions do differ, but try to persuade the judge that your opinion is to be preferred, given your reasoned argument.

FINDING OUT THE RESULT AFTER THE CASE IS OVER

If you stay until the end of the proceedings, in a criminal trial you will hear the verdict – guilty or not guilty. However, there will probably be an adjournment before sentencing; the judge will decide what sentence to give on a different day. In a civil trial, at the end of the trial the judge will give judgment (not a verdict).

If you are unable to stay until the end of the trial, ask the solicitors to let you know the outcome of the trial.

Do try to get some feedback from the instructing solicitors on how your evidence came across. You will have to ask them as they tend to be reluctant to give feedback.

Chapter 5

PAYMENT OF EXPERTS' FEES

SUMMARY
- Who pays the solicitor? ●
● Who is responsible for paying expert witnesses? ●
● How much will you be paid? ●
● When will you be paid? ●
● Cancellation fees ●
● VAT liability of medico-legal services ●

INTRODUCTION

Many expert witnesses experience problems in being paid for their services. This section aims to provide some guidance on the underlying principles concerning being paid. While there is no need for the expert to understand fully the system for payment of lawyers and experts in litigation, it is felt that a brief overview of this system may be of some assistance.

WHO PAYS THE SOLICITOR'S BILL?

The solicitor's bill, or "costs" as it is known in legal jargon, includes all the costs of the litigation incurred on behalf of the client who instructs them. This means the solicitor's own work, work done by barristers, experts' fees and any other expenses of the litigation.

In civil cases, the privately funded loser of a case may be ordered to pay some or all of the winner's costs. These are known as *inter partes* costs. Alternatively, the costs may be met by the Legal Aid Board. Thus, if a solicitor's client wins, the solicitor may be paid in total or in part by the client, the losing client or the Legal Aid Board.

Similarly, in criminal cases a defendant found guilty may be ordered to pay prosecution costs. If found not guilty, he may be awarded costs from central funds.

To a large extent, the method by which the solicitors get paid their costs, which include the experts' fees and expenses, is irrelevant to the expert witness. The expert witness has a contract with the solicitors who instruct him or her. This contract is binding, irrespective of how or when the solicitors themselves are paid.

TAXATION

In the case of all legally aided civil or criminal cases, and in the case of civil cases where there are inter partes costs paid by a privately funded losing party, these costs will be subject to taxation (in civil cases, or assessment in criminal cases). This means that the amount of costs incurred is looked at to see if it is appropriate and reasonable. Thus the lawyers' fees, counsels' fees, experts' fees and any other expenses are all looked at and the amount may be "taxed" or "assessed" down, until the fees are at a reasonable level. A taxing master (or justices' clerk in the Magistrates' Court) is the person responsible for deciding whether the fees are reasonable. The taxing master will look at the amount of time spent on any item and also the hourly rate charged.

PRIVATELY FUNDED CIVIL CASES

Who Is Responsible for Paying My Fees?

The contract is between you and the solicitor who instructs you. Solicitors will in most cases have asked their clients for funds on account to pay both your fees and your expenses (disbursements). Nevertheless, it is the solicitor who is liable to pay your fees, whether or not they have been given money on account by their clients.

Solicitors are responsible for paying for civil court attendance fees and expenses. They will receive the money from their own client or, if their client wins, the court may order the other side to pay some of the costs.

You are not to be paid directly by any other third party.

It is essential to consider carefully the terms of your contractual agreement with the solicitors before you undertake any work. The key terms are **how much** you are to be paid and **when** you will be paid.

How Much Will I Be Paid?

It is sensible to have a written contractual agreement with your instructing solicitors which sets out how much you will charge per hour, or per report. Your hourly rate will depend on the field of your expertise. It will also depend on whether you are using your expertise or merely travelling to meetings.

Keep a record of the date and the time you spend on any tasks. Also keep a record of any expenses you incur, e.g. travelling, photocopying, etc. A day to day record should be kept – see example overleaf.

It is best to have a contractual agreement that sets out that, irrespective of the outcome of any taxation hearing, the instructing solicitors must pay your fees in full. However, you may find solicitors reluctant to enter into such an agreement and they may require a modification to reflect payment according to the outcome of a taxation hearing.

Where your fees will be subject to taxation, it is crucial that you have records of the work you have undertaken so your instructing solicitors can justify to the taxing master the amount of your fees. The taxing master is the person who assesses what fees are reasonable.

Example of Time Record

File	Date	Time Spent	Task	Hourly Rate	Total
Jones	13th Sept 96	2 hrs	Reading papers	£90	£180
Jones	14th Sept 96	1 hr	Research	£100	£100
Jones	18th Sept 96	1.5 hrs	Examining patient	£100	£150
Jones	29th Sept 96	3 hrs	Meeting with counsel	£100	£300
Jones	3rd Oct 96	6 hrs	Writing report	£100	£600
Jones	1st Feb 97	1 hr	Travelling and waiting	£60	£60
Jones	1st Feb 97	2 hrs	In court	£100	£200
Expenses					

When Will I Receive My Fees and Expenses?

Have a term in your contract for services which states when payment is due – 14 days or 28 days after the date of the invoice. You are entitled to ask for expenses and fees on account, i.e. before they are incurred. However, it is common practice to send in an invoice for your fees and expenses once you have incurred them.

You should look carefully at your contractual agreement with the solicitors to see if you can get expenses/fees on account and whether you are entitled to interim payments. Interim payments are payments for fees and expenses as you proceed so that, at each stage of your work, you can ask for an interim payment on submission of your invoice. It may be possible to agree payment of expenses before they are incurred. Many experts send an invoice when they submit their report to the solicitors. Some even send the invoice before the report and will only send the report after they have been paid.

There is no need for you to wait until the litigation is over before submitting your invoice, particularly if you have agreed that your fees will be paid irrespective of the outcome of the litigation.

LEGALLY AIDED CIVIL CASES

Who Is Responsible for Paying My Fees?

As in privately funded cases, the solicitor who instructs you is responsible for payment of your fees. Payment depends on the terms of the contract between the solicitor and the expert. The Legal Aid Board pays the reasonable costs of the litigation to the solicitor who is under a contractual obligation to pay the expert's fees.

How Much Will I Be Paid?

Where the solicitor has agreed the fee, the expert will be paid in accordance with the contract and the solicitor must pay that full fee irrespective of whether this is more than the amount paid to the solicitor by the Legal Aid Board. Most experts prefer to agree fees in advance irrespective of the outcome of taxation, that is irrespective of any deductions from the fees made at a taxing hearing.

Prior Authority

Many solicitors will not wish to run the risk of being liable to pay the shortfall between what the Legal Aid Board pays them after taxation and the fee agreed with the expert. In this case, they will seek prior authority from the Legal Aid Board that it is necessary to instruct an expert and that the proposed fee is reasonable. Where such authority is granted, it will state the amount of expenditure on the expert's fees which is authorised. The effect of such prior authority is that the amount of the expert's fee will be guaranteed to be paid to the solicitor (with very limited exceptions). To help gain prior authority, the expert will be asked to provide a costed programme of work. If further work is required, then the Legal Aid Board's further authority must be sought for any additional fees and expenses.

When Will I Be Paid?

The timing of payment is also dependent on the terms of the contract between the solicitor and the expert. There is no implied term that the expert has to wait until the solicitor has been paid. The best terms are for the expert to be paid within 14/28 days of invoicing the solicitor. However, the solicitor may insist that payment should only be made within a reasonable time of the solicitor being paid on account by the Legal Aid Board. The expert must take a commercial decision as to whether the solicitor will instruct him/her if he/she insists on payment regardless of whether the solicitor is in funds from the Legal Aid Board.

It is important to note that it is *not* necessary to wait until the litigation has finished before the expert is paid. The solicitor can and should apply to the Legal Aid Board for payment on account of experts' fees and expenses incurred or about to be incurred. The expert witness should consider putting a clause in the contract with the solicitor to the effect that the solicitor will seek such payment on account from the Legal Aid Board.

PAYMENT FOR ATTENDANCE AT COURT IN CIVIL CASES

The solicitor who instructs the expert is responsible for paying all witnesses who attend court to give evidence. Again, prior authority for the fee to be paid can be obtained from the Legal Aid Board and payment on account can be obtained.

Cancellation Fees

There is no automatic payment of a fee where the expert's attendance at court is not required but the expert may obtain reasonably incurred expenses and/or payment for time spent in preparation. However, there is a duty to mitigate losses incurred, e.g. by rearranging appointments.

It is therefore wise to address the issue of how you will be compensated for cancellation of court appearances.

PRIVATELY FUNDED CRIMINAL CASES

The position for payment of experts is the same as in privately funded civil cases. Fees should be agreed in advance in the contract between the solicitor and the expert. Ideally, the expert should ask the solicitor to agree to pay the full amount irrespective of the outcome of any costs assessment.

LEGALLY AIDED CRIMINAL CASES

Who Is Responsible for Paying My Fees?

Again, the position is similar to civil cases. The instructing solicitor is responsible for paying the expert witness for everything, with the exception in this case of attendance at court.

How Much Will I Be Paid?

As in civil cases, the expert can agree the amount of his/her fees (apart from the attendance at court fee) with the instructing solicitor. The agreement can be for the full amount irrespective of any assessment down of the fee. However, as in civil cases, solicitors who are reluctant to face the risk of a deficit in the amount obtained after the assessment of costs by the Crown Court will apply for prior authorisation from the Legal Aid Board of the use of an expert and the amount of expenditure.

When Will I Be Paid?

In Crown Court cases, an interim payment/payment on account from the Crown Court can be made if the Legal Aid Board has authorised expenditure in excess of £100 and liability to pay a disbursement of £100 or more has arisen. Thus the solicitor needs:

(i) evidence of the prior authority; and

(ii) the expert's invoice.

There is no provision for payment on account in the Magistrates' Court.

PAYMENT FOR ATTENDANCE AT COURT IN CRIMINAL CASES

The rule in criminal cases is different from that in civil cases. This is, firstly, because payment is from central funds and, secondly, because there is no facility for obtaining prior authority or payment on account.

In criminal cases, central funds administered by the Lord Chancellor's department pay for the witness's attendance at court. This payment can be obtained by attending the court cash office after the witness has given evidence. There should be no delay in such payment, provided the expert's hourly rate is deemed reasonable. The amount allowed usually includes a notional one hour for preparation for the hearing.

For witnesses of fact or those classified for payment purposes as professional witnesses, payment is fixed by the Treasury. The allowances given are designed to compensate them for expenses or losses incurred in attending court to give evidence. For example, a general practitioner who has to attend court and therefore must hire in a locum can claim the expense of hiring the locum. For expert witnesses, the amount allowed will depend on their expertise and the nature and complexity of the case.

It may be disconcerting for expert witnesses to be unable to fix their fee for court attendance in criminal trials before they go to court. However, this problem cannot be avoided by refusing to attend court, since the solicitors would serve a witness summons on the expert. This obliges the expert to attend and failure to do so will amount to contempt of court and expose the witness to the risk of imprisonment.

Cancellation Fees

Where the court hearing is cancelled because the defendant pleads guilty, the expert witness may claim reasonably incurred expenses and/or preparation expenses. However, as in civil cases, there is a duty to mitigate the loss by rearranging appointments, etc.

VAT LIABILITY OF MEDICO-LEGAL SERVICES

Customs and Excise have made services where doctors are engaged *primarily* for work in the legal process subject to VAT; this was effective from 20th January 1997. This medico-legal work will usually be carried out at the instigation of third parties such as the patient's solicitors or an insurance company's solicitors. Typically, the work on which VAT is chargeable will be medical reports and services provided for the investigation of disputes between parties. The exemption from VAT continues to apply where a doctor is engaged in work arising from a normal patient/doctor relationship.

APPENDICES

PRO FORMA ENGAGEMENT LETTER
to be issued as soon as instructions or potential instructions are received

N.B. The Expert Witness Institute is in the process of drafting standard terms. These will be available in late 1997. This pro forma engagement letter, however, contains the essential elements.

```
Our ref:
Your ref:

                                      29 August 1997

Name and full address of
instructing solicitor's
firm – not an individual


Dear Sirs
```

<u>Case Name</u>

```
Thank you for your letter of instruction/potential
instruction dated ........

I set out below my understanding of the services
you require me to perform as an expert [accountant/
GP/surveyor/psychologist/nurse, etc.] in the above-
mentioned case.
```

Insert here a paragraph to explain what you have been engaged to do on this particular assignment; it is very important that you and the instructing solicitors are both aware of the scope of your advice. This

---

avoids later claims of negligence against you. It may fall within the following categories:

1. Preparation of a preliminary expert's report on quantum and/or liability.

   (A preliminary report is a report prepared for a solicitor to help the solicitor to decide if the solicitor's client, the plaintiff, has a case.)

2. Preparation of a final expert's report on quantum and/or liability.

   (This will usually take the form of an updated preliminary report, and will be on the same areas as 1. above.)

3. Preparation of a report for the defendant or the prosecution in a criminal case.

4. Attending meetings of experts to narrow the issues before trial.

5. Considering a settlement.

6. Attending conferences with counsel.

7. Attending at court for trial and/or other hearings.

Each case should be considered on its own merits and the paragraph describing the work that you are required to do should be drafted accordingly.

Obligations of the solicitor

1) Deal promptly with every reasonable request by me for authority to obtain any information and documents deemed by me necessary to fulfil your instructions.

2) Give prompt written notification of every meeting, hearing, trial or other appointment at which my attendance will be required.

3) Not alter or permit others to alter any of the reports produced by me.

4) Notify me in writing 7 days before disclosure of my report is to be made, so final checks to update the report can be made by me before the report is disclosed.

For civil cases:

5) The solicitor will provide me with all documents relevant to the case, in particular:

a) the plaintiff's/defendant's statements;

b) the plaintiff's statement of claim in the High Court, or particulars of claim in the County Court and, once the case has been started, any other pleadings;

c) all plaintiff and defendant witness statements;

d) the reports of other experts, for both the plaintiff and the defendant;

e) any directions of the court as to how the case is to be conducted;

f) any other relevant documents.

For criminal cases:

5) The solicitor will provide me with all the documents relevant to the case, and in particular:

a) notify me of what the defendant is charged with;

b) notify me what defence if any the defendant is relying on;

c) give me the defendant's statement;

d) give me witness statements for the prosecution and defence (or summaries);

e) give me reports of the expert witnesses for both the prosecution and the defence;

f) give me any other relevant documents.

Obligations of the expert

As the expert, I will:

a) use reasonable skill and care in the performance of the instructions given to me;

b) act with objectivity and independence with regard to my instructions and, in the event of a conflict between my duties to your client and to the court, hold my duties to the court paramount;

c) undertake only those parts of a case in respect of which I consider I have adequate qualifications and experience;

d) promptly notify the solicitor of any matter (including a conflict of interest or lack of suitable qualifications and experience) which would disqualify me or render it undesirable for me to have continued involvement in the case;

e) use all reasonable endeavours to make myself available for all meetings, hearings, trials and other appointments of which I have received adequate written notice;

f) not without good cause discharge myself from the appointment as expert;

g) preserve confidentiality save as expressly or by necessary implication authorised to the contrary;

h) not negotiate with another party or adviser unless specifically authorised by the solicitor to do so. For avoidance of doubt this does not apply to any order of a court or tribunal.

Intellectual property rights

The rights of ownership in respect of all documents, photographic negatives, video recordings, models and other original work created by me shall remain vested in me unless otherwise agreed in writing.

Fees

My fees are based upon the degree of responsibility and skill involved and the time necessarily occupied on the work. Unless otherwise agreed, they will be charged separately for each class of work mentioned above. For example, my hourly rate for preparation of evidence is £—. My daily rate for attending a hearing is £—. I will also invoice you for any reasonable costs incurred.

Invoices for work done will be rendered at appropriate times.

Initial review of cases

I am prepared on request to undertake an initial review of any case in which instructing solicitors consider that I may be able to assist. I am prepared to set out in writing how I may be able to help, and to give an indication of my likely fee. In legal aid cases, I will provide a costed programme of work in a form suitable for production by instructing solicitors to the Legal Aid Board for prior authority.

My time spent on that initial review is costed in the fee indicator or the costed programme of work.

If for any reason my potential appointment is not confirmed, there will be no charge for this initial review unless prior agreement on charges has been reached between myself and yourselves, the instructing solicitors.

Legal aid funded cases

In cases where my fees are to be funded by the Legal Aid Board, I will provide a costed programme of work and require you to obtain its approval (prior authority) by the Legal Aid Board. I wish to receive a copy of the form of approval, before any work is undertaken. I reserve the right to approach the Legal Aid Board through you for prior approval of fees to complete the work, or to undertake additional work, should this prove necessary.

Where a fee has been agreed in advance with the Legal Aid Board or your client, I reserve the right to invoice the full cost of my fees even if this exceeds the fee agreed in advance.

Insert here 1) or 2) below; 1) is more favourable for solicitors but may be necessary for you to secure the work.

1) I will not demand payment of that excess until the conclusion of the case, at which stage all or part of that excess will be cancelled if it

is not recovered by instructing solicitors, at taxation of costs or otherwise.

2) Irrespective of when or indeed if instructing solicitors receive payment from the Legal Aid Board, my fees shall be paid within 14 days of the date of my invoice.

Instructing solicitors will apply promptly to the Legal Aid Board for interim payments of my fees and disbursements as invoiced, and will remit promptly to me all such payments received.

Instructing solicitors will also use their best endeavours to ensure that:

(i)   my personal expenses are paid on account;

(ii)   where a taxation/assessment of costs is necessary, it will be applied for, pursued or defended (as appropriate) in a timely manner, and that

(iii) my reasonable fees and disbursements are recovered in full by way of the Legal Aid Fund.

Privately funded cases

In privately funded cases, the instructing solicitors will at all times ensure that they are in funds to discharge and that they do promptly discharge my fees and disbursements [within e.g. 21 days/28 days of date of invoice], unless specifically agreed otherwise. I remind you that you remain liable to pay my invoice even if your client has not paid you. My full fees are to be paid irrespective of the outcome of any taxation of costs.

I reserve the right to charge interest at 3% above Lloyds Bank base rates on overdue amounts.

Once it has been agreed, this letter will remain effective until it is replaced.

I shall be obliged if you will acknowledge acceptance of the terms of this letter by signing the duplicate copy and returning it to me, keeping the first copy with your records.

If the contents are not in accordance with your understanding of our agreement, I shall be pleased to receive your further observations and to give you any further information you require.

Yours faithfully

THE ABOVE TERMS AND CONDITIONS ARE AGREED

Signed.................................

Position...............................

Firm..................................

Date..................................

MODEL REPORT

XXXXXXXX V XXXXXXXX
[Title of the action]

XXXXXXXXXX
[Court reference number]

FINAL REPORT OF *[your name]* **FOR THE** *[name of the court]*

Dated: *[The date you sign your report and send it to your instructing solicitors]*

Specialist field: *[Your specialist field]*

On behalf of *[the plaintiff/defendant]*: *[The name of the party to the action]*

On the instructions of: *[The name of the solicitors who have instructed you]*

Subject matter: *[A very brief description of the subject matter]*

This format is only a **suggestion.** *It contains the main elements you will need to consider but you will need to create your own personal format that will depend on your specialist field and the particular case. This front page should be visible, preferably with a transparent plastic sheet, although this is optional. Do not use comb binders. Use A4 good quality paper, hole punched for lever arch files with a slide binder. Find out from the solicitors who instruct you how many top copies are needed. The report is addressed to the court as Lord Woolf has recommended.*

[Your]
Name:
Address:
Telephone number:
Fax number:
Reference:

Report of *[your name]*   *Page 2*
Specialist field *[your specialist field]*
On behalf of *[the plaintiff/defendant – name of the party you have been instructed by]*

CONTENTS

Paragraph number	*Paragraph contents*	*Page number*
1	Introduction	
2	The issues addressed	
3	My investigation of the facts	
4	My opinion	

Appendices

1	Details of my qualifications and experience	
2	Documents that I have examined, with copies of important documents	
3	Published material referred to, with copies of extracts	
4	Photographs and diagrams	
5	Chronology	
6	Glossary of technical terms	
7	Lord Woolf declaration and instructions	
8	Other	

This contents page is useful even if the report is short. In longer reports, the contents page may need to be more detailed so the reader can easily find their way around the report.

Report of *[your name]*   *Page 3*
Specialist field *[your specialist field]*
On behalf of *[the plaintiff/defendant – name of the party you have been instructed by]*

REPORT

1 Introduction

1.01 The writer

I am *[your full name]*. My specialist field is *[your specialist field and give a short summary of the most important qualifications and experience relevant to the case – no more than three lines]*.

Full details of my qualifications and experience entitling me to give expert opinion evidence are in Appendix 1. *[It is necessary to have these full details as you may be cross-examined on them.]*

1.02 Summary of the case

The case concerns *[give a short outline of the case]*. There is a chronology of the key events in Appendix 5. I have been instructed to *[say briefly what you have been asked to do]*.

1.03 Summary of my conclusions

This report will show that in my professional opinion *[give your conclusion. It is good practice to put an "executive" summary at the beginning so that the reader knows the direction of your analysis]*.

1.04 The parties involved

Those involved in the case are as follows:

[List the people and organisations you refer to in your report with a short description of each. This can be very useful for a judge.]

1.05 Technical terms and explanations

I have indicated any technical terms in **bold type.** I have defined these

Report of *[your name]*   *Page 4*
Specialist field *[your specialist field]*
On behalf of *[the plaintiff/defendant – name of the party you have been instructed by]*

terms when first used and included them in a glossary in Appendix 6. I have also included in Appendix 3 extracts of published works I refer to in my report and in Appendix 4 there are diagrams and photographs to assist in the understanding of the case.

Report of *[your name]*
Specialist field *[your specialist field]*
On behalf of *[the plaintiff/defendant – name of the party you have been instructed by]*

2   The issues addressed

2.01   *[Set out the issues you will address in your report. Number each issue as you will refer to each in your opinion in paragraph 4. Do not give your opinion here.]*

***Report of** [your name]*   *Page 6*
***Specialist field** [your specialist field]*
***On behalf of** [the plaintiff/defendant – name of the party you have been instructed by]*

3   My investigation of the facts

[This section establishes the foundation of fact upon which you will base your opinion. The starting point is "I do not know, but let me see what the facts are". Set out the facts of the case as you see them. Identify the source of these facts. You must distinguish fact from opinion. Also distinguish facts you have been told and those you personally observed. This paragraph is purely factual. Paragraph 4 will deal with your opinion.]

3.01   Documents

[Identify the important documents for the judge. Remember that Appendix 2 contains a list of the documents you have considered with copies of the really important ones.]

3.02   Interviews and examinations

[Give details of any interviews and examinations you did. Give dates and times. Say if anyone else was present. There may be none.]

3.03   Research

[Give details of any research papers you considered. Remember that Appendix 3 contains a list of published works you refer to and has copy extracts. Lord Woolf has recommended that, as an expert, you should give details of any literature or other material which you have used in making your report.]

3.04   Experiments, etc.

[Give details of any experiments you did to prepare for the report. You should say who carried out any test or experiment which you use in your report and give their qualifications.]

Report of *[your name]*
Specialist field [your specialist field]
On behalf of *[the plaintiff/defendant – name of the party you have been instructed by]*

Page 7

4 My opinion

[Go through each issue identified in Paragraph 2, link these to the facts from Paragraph 3 and then give your reasoned argument for the opinion you come to.

Facts, analysis then argued conclusion.

*Remember, the reader of your report does not have your knowledge and expertise. They need to have your thinking **explained**. Avoid using the word negligence as this is a legal term. Let the judge make the decision, so just give your professional opinion. Do not give a legal opinion.*

Lord Woolf has recommended that, where there is a range of opinion on the matters dealt with in your report, summarise this range of opinion and give your reasons for your opinion.]

Signature .... **Date** ....

[Do not forget to sign and date your report!]

Report of *[your name]*   *Page 8*
Specialist field *[your specialist field]*
On behalf of *[the plaintiff/defendant – name of the party you have been instructed by]*

Appendix 1

Details of my qualifications and experience

This is the front sheet for the contents of the appendix. Have a separate sheet for each appendix.

Report of *[your name]*
Specialist field *[your specialist field]*
On behalf of *[the plaintiff/defendant – name of the party you have been instructed by]*

Page 9

Appendix 7

Lord Woolf declaration and instructions

This declaration is based on rule 32 of the Draft Civil Proceedings Rules of the Lord Woolf Access to Justice enquiry. You will need to copy your instructions and attach them to your report.

Lord Woolf Declaration

a) I understand that my duty as an expert witness is to the court.

b) I have complied with that duty.

c) This report includes all matters relevant to the issues on which my expert evidence is given.

d) I have given details in this report of any matters which might affect the validity of this report.

e) I have addressed this report to the court.

f) I have attached to this report:

1) All written instructions given to me.

2) Any supplemental written instructions given to me since the original instructions were given.

3) A note of any oral instructions given to me.

HERE IS A CHECK LIST TO USE WHEN YOU HAVE
COMPLETED YOUR REPORT

yes	no	
✓	✓	
❑	❑	A4 good quality paper, hole punched for lever arch file
❑	❑	Chronology
❑	❑	Clear headings
❑	❑	Contents page
❑	❑	Covering letter and invoice
❑	❑	Dated
❑	❑	Double spaced or space and a half
❑	❑	Expressed in the first person
❑	❑	Front sheet
❑	❑	Glossary
❑	❑	Graphics
❑	❑	Headers on each page
❑	❑	Margins wide enough for written comments
❑	❑	Pages numbered
❑	❑	Paragraphs numbered
❑	❑	Publications dated and precede incident date (if appropriate)
❑	❑	Short sentences and paragraphs
❑	❑	Signed
❑	❑	Synopsis

Review the following pointers:

✓

❑   Accurate?

❑   Clear conclusion?

❑   Fact and opinion clearly separated?

❑   Good use of appendices?

❑   How concise is the report?

❑   How clearly are the issues identified?

❑   How clear is the language for a non expert to read?

❑   How logical is the report?

❑   How far does the report stand alone, i.e. contains everything that the judge would need?

❑   How well are the qualifications and experience set out?

❑   Quality of paper?

❑   Quality of printing?

❑   *EASY for judges and lawyers to use?!*

Appendix 3

ACCESS TO JUSTICE – THE LORD WOOLF ENQUIRY

INTRODUCTION

It has always been the case that by definition, experts should be independent. Under the recommendations, they must be seen to be independent. The days of the hired gun may be numbered. Woolf has said he intends to increase the independence of experts and to reduce their partisan use by the parties.

Woolf expressed concern that some experts failed to maintain their independence from the party by whom they had been instructed. He indicated there were several different roles and functions that experts can play. They can:

- Assist a party to establish the facts and to assess the merits of a case.

- Give expert opinion evidence to the court.

- Give factual evidence to the court.

- Conduct inquiries on behalf of the court.

- Sit with a judge to help understanding of technical matters.

The proposal of a single court appointed expert met with considerable resistance from lawyers in the consultation process. Lord Woolf said "It is clear that the idea is anathema to many members of the legal profession in this country who are reluctant to give up their adversarial weapons (*sic*)." He proposes that although experts should all be "neutral" they could still function within a broad adversarial framework. Wherever possible, the expert should be chosen by agreement between the parties and should act on instructions from the parties. He found widespread agreement with the criticism that experts sometimes take on the role of partisan advocates instead of neutral finders or opinion givers. The basic premise of his new approach is that the expert's function is to help the court.

Woolf's overriding principle that the courts should be in charge of the management of cases also applies to experts. There should be no expert evidence at all unless it will help the court. There should be no more than one expert in any one speciality unless there is a real purpose.

The new rules will not allow expert evidence without leave. The options will be:

● No experts.

● A limited number of experts.

● One or more experts chosen by agreement between the parties or appointed by the court.

● Written expert evidence only.

Transparent Instructions

To emphasise the role of independent adviser, reports intended for use as evidence in court proceedings should be addressed to the court and instructions should be "transparent". The interim report went as far as to suggest that legal privilege should not apply to communications between the expert and the client and legal advisers. The Final Report does not follow this but does remove privilege from the instructions, so solicitors will need to be particularly thoughtful in their instructions. The Report goes on to say that reports should contain a declaration that includes that: the expert understands his primary duty is to the court; the report is accurate and complete and mentions all material matters including anything that may adversely affect his opinion; and his opinion is independent.

Experts' Meetings

Woolf wants the issues in cases involving experts to be narrowed by the experts in meetings. A principle recommendation is that opposing experts should adopt a co-operative approach. Wherever possible, there should be a joint investigation and a single report that indicates areas of disagreement. Lord Woolf found that the present system does not encourage narrowing of issues between opposing experts or the elimination of peripheral issues. He found experts are sometimes instructed not to agree anything or that any points of agreement must be ratified by the lawyers. He recommends experts should meet in private and produce for the court a written list of agreed matters of professional opinion and matters in dispute. However, it is still for the parties and their legal advisers to consider the effect of any agreement or disagreement on the future conduct of the case. It will be more important than ever that an expert knows what is expected of them. Woolf has suggested that in some cases the agenda for the expert's meeting should be set by the court and define the subject matter to be covered. The report also emphasised that the experts should communicate as soon as possible. The earlier an expert is instructed, the better.

The Report found much concern over the quality and reliability of experts' reports. Problems included: reports that were partisan, contained irrelevant material, strayed outside the expert field or missed the issues to be considered. It seems many experts do not understand their role or how to produce effective evidence. Lord Woolf states "I certainly support the provision of training for experts, both through attendance at courses and through the dissemination of published material". He does not recommend an exclusive system of accreditation as this could exclude potentially competent experts. The days of the amateur expert are numbered; the courts and solicitors will require experts to understand their role.

The role of the expert has not fundamentally changed as a result of the Report. However, independence must not only be done but must be seen to be done. The expert must now seek common ground with the other expert in a case and must remember the primary duty is to the court.

EXTRACTS FROM THE WOOLF REPORT (Paragraphs 30-51)

30. There was wide support for the proposal in my interim report that an expert's report intended for use as evidence in court proceedings should be addressed to the court. I now propose that there should be a requirement to this effect in the rules of court to apply whenever litigation is contemplated. This is a formal but important requirement. It does not imply that the expert is to be instructed by the court, but is intended to concentrate the expert's mind as he writes the report on his paramount duty to the court.

31. One of the recommendations in my interim report was that, once an expert had been instructed to prepare a report for the use of a court, any communication between the expert and the client or his advisers should no longer be the subject of legal privilege. My intention was to prevent the suppression of relevant opinions or factual material which did not support the case put forward by the party instructing the expert. There is, I believe, no disagreement with that intention, but it has been put to me very strongly that waiver of legal privilege is not the way to achieve it. The point has been made

that experts must be free to submit drafts to clients and their legal advisers, so that factual misconceptions can be corrected. A further objection is that a great deal of time could be wasted if all these documents were disclosable, because the opposing party would have to comb through the various versions of a report to identify any changes, the reasons for which would not always be clear in any event. Another possibility is that lawyers and experts might begin to subvert the system by avoiding written communication in favour of off the record conversations.

32. I accept, in the light of these arguments, that it would not be realistic to make draft experts' reports disclosable. I do not, however, consider that privilege should apply to the instructions given to experts. The Chancery Working Group has pointed out that major problems can arise when opposing experts are working from different instructions, which leads to reports that are hard to compare and use. Joint or agreed instructions would meet this specific point, but even a single expert's report may be unclear or open to misinterpretation unless the instructions on which it is based are known.

33. Under the new system, transparency of instructions to experts will be particularly important. The effectiveness of pre-action protocols will depend on it. On the fast track, in cases where there are diverging opinions in two reports, it will be absolutely essential for the parties and the judge to know the basis on which the experts have been instructed. I therefore recommend that expert evidence should not be admissible unless all written instructions (including letters subsequent upon the original instructions) and a note of any oral instructions are included as an annex to the expert's report.

34. A further recommendation in the interim report was that any expert's report prepared for the purpose of giving evidence to a court should end with a declaration that it includes everything which the expert

regards as being relevant to the opinion which he has expressed in his report and that he has drawn to the attention of the court any matter which would affect the validity of that opinion. That recommendation was widely supported on consultation, and I have come to the conclusion that a declaration along the lines I have proposed, coupled with the requirement for instructions to be disclosed, should be sufficient to meet my concerns about the disclosure of all relevant material.

35. The Working Group on Intellectual Property has proposed a form of declaration which would include statements that the expert:

(a) understands that his primary duty is to the court, both in preparing his report and in giving evidence;

(b) has endeavoured in his report to be accurate and complete, and to mention all matters which he regards as being material to the opinions he has expressed;

(c) has drawn the court's attention to any matter of which he is aware which might adversely affect the validity of his opinions;

(d) has indicated the source of his factual information if he has based an opinion on facts of which he has no personal knowledge;

(e) has not included anything in the report which has been suggested to him by anyone (including particularly his instructing lawyers) without forming his own independent view on the matter;

(f) will notify his instructing lawyers immediately in writing if for any reason he considers that his existing report requires any correction or qualification; and, if the correction or qualification is significant, will prepare a supplementary report as soon as possible; and

(g) understands that

(i) his report will form the evidence he will give under oath, subject to any corrections he may make before swearing as to its correctness;

(ii) he may be cross-examined on his report by a cross-examiner assisted by an expert; and

(iii) if the court concludes that he has not fairly tried to meet the standards set out in the declaration, he is likely to be the subject of public adverse criticism by the judge.

36. I should like to see added to this a statement that where there is a range of reasonable opinion, the expert has indicated the extent of that range in his report.

37. Some elements in the working group's suggested declaration may be controversial; in particular, it might be argued that a reference to the possibility of adverse criticism could deter competent experts from giving evidence. I believe, however, that the outline broadly sets out the points which should be included in an expert's declaration. It could usefully form the basis of discussion between the Law Society, the Academy of Experts and any other interested bodies, with a view to drawing up a standard declaration for use in experts' reports.

Access to Evidence: Inequality of Resources

38. One of the fundamental principles of my approach to civil litigation is that there should, so far as possible, be a level playing field between litigants of unequal financial or other resources. A particular problem arises when one party, often the defendant or potential defendant, has an easily available source of expertise to which the other party does not have access. This happens, for example, in medical negligence, where a health authority or hospital

trust can use its own doctors; or in actions against large companies with in-house technical experts. The potential claimant, on the other hand, may not even know whether he or she has a case worth pursuing without paying for an independent expert to carry out an investigation.

39. I suggested in the issues paper that one way of redressing this imbalance would be to introduce a new procedure enabling claimants to apply to the court (either before or after proceedings have started) for an order requiring the defendant to provide an in-house expert's report on a particular situation. It seemed to me that such a procedure would be particularly helpful to claimants who did not qualify for legal aid, although it could also save money for the Legal Aid Fund. The provision of an in-house report would not prevent the opposing party from instructing his or her own expert at a later stage if it emerged that there was a case worth pursuing.

40. This proposal was generally opposed by respondents to the consultation paper. Prospective defendants considered it unfair, and claimants' representatives questioned whether an in-house report could be accepted as impartial and independent, because of the fear that an in-house expert would come under pressure to report in favour of the defendant. In the light of this reaction, I have considered whether there may be a more acceptable way of achieving my objective than a specific power to direct a prospective defendant to carry out investigations or tests.

41. I have concluded that the court should have a wide power, which could be exercised before the start of proceedings, to order that an examination or tests should be carried out in relation to any matter in issue, and a report submitted to the court. Any such order would indicate by whom the examination or tests were to be carried out, and at whose cost. This will cover a wider range of situations than I originally had in mind, and can be applied flexibly by the courts to meet particular circumstances.

Narrowing the Issues: Experts' Meetings

42. Among the criticisms I made in my interim report was that the present system does not encourage narrowing of issues between opposing experts, or the elimination of peripheral issues. There has been widespread support for my suggestion that experts' meetings were a useful approach to narrowing the issues. In areas of litigation (such as Official Referees' business) where experts' meetings are already the usual practice, there is general agreement that they are helpful. In areas where they are not at present widely used, including medical negligence, the majority of respondents accept that they could be helpful. (This is not, however, the view of the Intellectual Property Working Group, which believes that sequential disclosure of reports may be a better way of narrowing the issues in some cases, or that each expert might usefully be asked to take the opposite side's report and underline the passages with which he or she disagrees.)

43. Two principal reservations have been expressed, even by those who support experts' meetings in principle. The first (mentioned in my interim report) is that meetings can be futile because the experts are instructed not to agree anything; or, alternatively, are told that any points of agreement must be referred back to their instructing lawyers for ratification. This subverts the judge's intention in directing the experts to meet, because the decision as to what to agree becomes a matter for the lawyers rather than the experts. I recommended in the interim report that it should be unprofessional conduct for an expert to be given or to accept instructions not to agree, and this has been widely supported.

44. On the basis of the consultation I have carried out, it is far from clear whether these are widespread problems, although there is certainly evidence that they do happen on occasions. The solution lies in a clear requirement that the experts must produce for the court, at the

end of their meeting, a written list of agreed matters of professional opinion and issues still in dispute. It must be made clear that the discussion is to cover only matters within the experts' professional competence, and that it is for the parties and their legal advisers to consider the effect of any agreement or disagreement on the future conduct of the case.

45. At least in the heaviest cases where expert issues are likely to be most complex, the agenda for the experts' meeting should be set by the court. Narrowing the issues to be put before the court, including issues of expert opinion, is one of the fundamental purposes of the system of case management I have proposed. The procedural judge conducting a case management conference should not only direct an experts' meeting but define (with the help of the parties and their legal advisers) the subject matter to be covered.

46. The second reservation about the need for experts' meetings relates to cost. It is said that meetings are expensive to set up, especially if they are attended by the parties' legal advisers. My answer to this point is that, provided a clear agenda is set and the meeting is properly conducted, the investment, in the vast majority of cases, will be well worthwhile. Where the meeting does not lead directly to settlement, it will reduce the scope of further work on the case and either facilitate settlement at a later stage or ensure that the trial focuses on the essential issues. In any event, the net result should be a saving of costs.

47. It is also worth pointing out that, at least in the more straightforward cases, it may be possible to hold a 'meeting' by using telephone conferencing and video conferencing technologies, at less expense than bringing the experts physically together. The important point is that they communicate with each other.

48. It is important, too, that experts communicate at the earliest possible stage in the case, to establish that they are answering the same

questions or addressing the same issues. A useful starting point for discussions between experts would be to prepare an agreed chronology and statement of facts, with a summary of important or disputed points. This should be done as soon as possible after submission of the defence, with a view to identifying non-contentious points from the outset so as to define the scope of the experts' reports. In some cases, the first meeting may be only after the exchange of experts' reports. At that stage, in any event, the reports themselves will provide a clear and agreed basis for the discussion.

49. In areas of litigation where the use of experts' meetings is well established, it seems to be accepted that there is no difficulty in allowing them to be conducted in private, with no-one present apart from the experts themselves. In other areas, it has been suggested that experts' meetings should take place only in the presence of the parties' lawyers, or of a neutral third party such as an independent lawyer or the procedural judge. In medical negligence, for example, it is thought that such an arrangement would be needed to overcome the traditional attitude of suspicion between the parties. In particular, it is said that private meetings between experts would not be acceptable to patients, because of the common perception that doctors 'hang together'.

50. In the majority of cases I see no reason why the experts should not meet alone, but I accept that there are circumstances in which this will not be appropriate. When the court directs a meeting, I suggest that the onus should be on the parties to apply for any special arrangements. In considering any such application, the court should bear in mind the expense of attendance by the parties' lawyers. When the lawyers do attend, it must also be made clear that they are present simply as observers to ensure fair play, and not to participate in the discussion or inhibit legitimate agreement between the experts.

51. Given the potential advantages, and the flexibility of the possible arrangements, it is difficult to see why there should not be at least one experts' meeting in all cases where opposing experts are involved. Certainly, I would not expect to see any substantial case come to trial under the new system without at least one such meeting having taken place.

GLOSSARY
of some common legal terms

Action
Civil legal proceedings.

Admissible evidence
Evidence that is permitted to be heard or read in court and taken into account.

Adversarial system
The method of deciding cases in court whereby the opposing parties argue their standpoints.

Advocate
A lawyer who pleads the case of his/her client. (A witness is not an advocate.)

Affirmation
A non-religious alternative to the oath but of equal weight. A witness lying after affirming in court is liable to be charged with perjury.

Alternative dispute resolution (ADR)
A process outside the litigation system for negotiating a settlement in which a third party acts as a mediator but has no power to make a decision that is legally binding on the parties.

Appeal
Proceedings taken in a higher court to overturn a lower court's decision in a case on the grounds that it was erroneously made or incorrect in law.

Arbitration
An adjudication process operating outside the court structure. The decision of the arbitrator is legally binding. Arbitration may be ordered by the court or agreed to by the parties.

Barrister
A qualified lawyer who is a member of one of the four Inns of Court and has been called to the bar. Barristers can work in all courts and are instructed by solicitors, not members of the public. They are self-employed, work from offices called chambers and wear wigs and gowns in court (other than in the Magistrates' Court).

Bar vocational course
A one year academic and practical course with exams at the end which enables a person to qualify as a barrister. This is undertaken by law

graduates or non-law graduates who have passed the Common
Professional Exam. A further one year's pupillage (training with a senior
barrister) is necessary before they can work as self-employed barristers.

Brief

The document summarising a case that is prepared by a solicitor and sent
to the barrister in order that he may advise on the case and, if necessary,
subsequently appear in court.

Burden and standard of proof

Having the burden of proof means that party must be the one to prove their
case. The standard of proof is the level of proof that must be demonstrated
by a party for the court to rule in their favour. In civil cases this level is 'on
the balance of probabilities', while in criminal cases it is 'beyond reasonable
doubt'.

Case

A particular legal proceeding.

Causation

The relationship between cause and effect.

Civil case

A dispute between two parties in which one seeks redress from the other.

Client

A member of the public who instructs a solicitor to act on their behalf.

Common Professional Exam (CPE)

An exam taken by non-law graduates at the end of an intensive year
studying law. It is the first stage in going on to become a solicitor or
barrister.

Compensation

Payment to an injured party as redress for the injury, damage or loss
suffered.

Conduct money

The money repaid to a witness of fact for the cost of public transport from
home to court, plus a fee and any loss of pay.

Conference

A meeting between a barrister and the solicitor, client or witness.

Contemporaneous note

A record or note made by a witness at the time of the event happening or
shortly afterwards while it was still fresh in the mind.

Counsel

A barrister.

Counterclaim

A claim by the defendant in a civil case that the plaintiff has caused the defendant a loss or damages, rather than the other way round.

County Court

A civil court where the lower value claims for damages by a plaintiff are heard.

Court bundle

All the documents relevant to the case in court. They are ordered and numbered and are available for witnesses to look at in court.

Criminal case

A case brought on behalf of the State against an individual who has broken the criminal law.

Cross-examination

The questioning of a witness by the party who did not call them, with the object of discrediting their evidence.

Crown Court

A criminal court with a judge and jury. The jury decides if the defendant is guilty or not guilty. The most serious criminal offences are heard in the Crown Court.

Crown Prosecution Service (CPS)

The organisation that brings prosecutions on behalf of the State.

Damages

Money paid as compensation.

Decision

The judgment of the court.

Defendant

In civil trials: the person sued. In criminal trials: the person accused of a crime.

Discovery/disclosure

The showing of each party's evidence to the other before a trial to ensure that there is no surprise or 'ambush' evidence presented at the trial. Experts' final reports for use at a trial must be disclosed to the other party.

Either way offences

Criminal offences which may be tried either in the Crown Court or the Magistrates' Court.

Evidence

The means by which something is proved. Written evidence may comprise statements or reports or other documents. Oral evidence is the spoken evidence of witnesses in court.

Examination in chief
The first questions asked of a witness in court by the lawyer representing the party who has asked that witness to give evidence.

Exchange of pleadings
The swapping between the parties of the formal documents that each party has produced setting out their view of the case.

Expert witness
Non-lawyer specialists in a particular field who are asked by solicitors to give an independent opinion on aspects of a case. Their role in court is to help the decision-maker(s) (judge/jury/magistrates) to understand the case.

Further and better particulars
More details about a case requested by the opposing party.

Hearsay
What someone has overheard or been told happened rather than what they saw happen themselves. Hearsay evidence, being 'second-hand', is usually inadmissible.

High Court
A civil court where the higher value claims are heard.

Indictable only
A criminal offence which is of a serious nature and the trial of which must take place in the Crown Court.

Indictment
The document which sets out the charge against a defendant in serious offences.

Injury
Physical injury, loss or damage.

Inspection
The looking at documents and reports of the opposing party prior to the case.

Inter partes costs
Costs paid by the loser to the winner in a civil case.

Issue of proceedings
The formal process by which a plaintiff starts litigation in the court system.

Judgment
The decision or sentence of the court.

Jury
Twelve members of the public who decide whether a defendant in a

criminal trial is guilty or not based on the evidence presented in court. Juries are also used in a limited number of civil cases to decide between the parties.

Lawyer

A barrister or solicitor.

Legal aid

Taxpayers' money available to help to pay the costs of court cases for those who cannot afford them.

Legal Practice Course (LPC)

A one year course of academic and practical study, with exams, taken by law graduates or those who are non-law graduates but who have passed the Common Professional Exam. Passing the LPC is the first stage in becoming a solicitor. A further two years' training at a solicitors firm is necessary before the person becomes a solicitor.

Letter before action

A letter sent by the plaintiff's solicitor to the defendant threatening litigation if settlement is not made.

Liability

The responsibility for an action or an event that results in loss or damage.

Magistrate

A lay Justice of the Peace who sits with one or two others to try cases in the Magistrates' Court. A stipendiary magistrate is a legally qualified paid Justice who sits alone.

Magistrates' Court

The lowest criminal court. All cases start here and, depending on their seriousness, are either tried by the magistrates or sent to a higher court. Decisions as to bail are also made. Other responsibilities of Magistrates' Courts include licensing and family matters.

Negligence

A failure of duty of care that results in loss or injury.

Oath

A formal religious declaration made by a witness before they give their evidence to say that they will tell the truth. If a witness lies having taken an oath in court, they may be charged with perjury. An oath carries the same weight as an affirmation.

Opinion evidence

The view of an independent expert in a specialist field on the facts of a case.

Particulars of claim

A formal document produced by the plaintiff in a civil case setting out their view of the case and what they want if they win.

Party

One of the 'sides' in a case, i.e. the plaintiff or the defendant. There may also be a third party involved.

Payment into court

A sum of money paid to the court by a defendant as an offer to settle a civil case. If accepted by the plaintiff, the case ends. If not accepted and the plaintiff wins but is awarded a lower sum in damages, the plaintiff becomes liable for all the legal costs of the case.

Plaintiff

The person who sues a defendant for damages in a civil case.

Pleading

A formal document that each party produces setting out their view of the case.

Preliminary report

A report by an expert witness to enable the plaintiff's solicitor to decide if the plaintiff has a worthwhile case to bring against the defendant.

Privilege

The protection from general public knowledge of a document, statement or report, which was prepared for the purpose of litigation.

Privilege is lost once the party has decided that a piece of evidence is going to be used at trial. The evidence is then disclosed/revealed to the other party. Any document, statement or report which is not going to be used at trial may remain privileged; it is confidential to the solicitors, the client and the expert witness (if applicable).

Professional witness

A witness who gives evidence as a result of seeing or doing something in the course of their everyday job; for example, police officers or police surgeons. These witnesses give mainly factual evidence, but can give opinion evidence in areas within their specialist field of knowledge. They are classified separately from expert witnesses for the purpose of payment by the Legal Aid Board.

Prosecution

The bringing of a criminal case against a defendant. A prosecution is usually brought on behalf of the State by the Crown Prosecution Service but may be brought by a private individual or body in the form of a private prosecution.

Quantum

Amount (of money by way of compensation/damages).

Queen's Counsel (QC)

A senior barrister who usually has 20 or more years' experience. Sometimes known as a "silk" or "leading counsel".

Re-examination

The third set of questions asked of a witness in court by the lawyer representing the party who has asked that witness to give evidence. It follows the examination in chief and the cross-examination. The intention is allow the witness to say things to improve the client's case by mending any damage done by the cross-examination.

Res ipsa loquitur

A Latin phrase meaning *the thing speaks for itself.* A party may suggest that the only way something could have occurred was if the other party was negligent.

Section 9 statement (Criminal Justice Act 1967)

A witness statement that is accepted by the opposing party. This lack of objection allows the statement to be read in court without the need for the witness to give oral evidence and be cross-examined.

Setting down for trial

The fixing of the date for a trial.

Settlement

An agreement between the parties to end a case without going to the very end of a trial.

Silk

Queen's Counsel, a senior barrister.

Solicitor

A qualified lawyer who may be instructed directly by members of the public. Solicitors may appear in certain courts but ask barristers to appear for them in higher courts. They are either self-employed or work in partnerships (called practices) and they do not wear wigs in court.

Statement of claim

A formal document produced by the plaintiff for use in the High Court giving their view of the case and what they want if they win.

Summary only offence

A criminal offence of a minor nature that can be tried only in the Magistrates' Court.

Summary trial
A criminal trial which takes place in the Magistrates' Court.

Taxation
The process by which a taxing master (an adjudicator) or justices' clerk decides what are fair and reasonable fees for solicitors and expert witnesses. Fees may be taxed down, that is, reduced, if the taxing master or justices' clerk considers that too much time was spent on an item or the hourly rate charged was too high.

Terms and conditions
The details of the contract between an expert witness and the solicitor who has instructed him/her, including the solicitors' obligations and when and how the expert is to be paid.

Trial
A court hearing to decide whether or not a defendant is guilty in a criminal case or which party wins in a civil case.

Vicarious liability
The legal liability of a person or organisation for the acts of another, e.g. a health authority may be liable for the work done by a doctor employed by them.

Without prejudice
Without prejudging an issue. Without prejudice negotiations may take place between parties which, if unsuccessful, will not have a bearing on the court case as anything discussed will be inadmissible in court.

Witness of fact
A person who has seen or heard something themselves and gives evidence in court.

Witness summons/subpoena
A written order by the court demanding the attendance of a witness at court. Non attendance will be contempt of court and may result in imprisonment.

Writ
A formal document prepared by the plaintiff to start a civil case in the High Court.